P9-BXZ-010

Richard Peace

NOTICING GOD

in mystical encounters

in the ordinary

in the still small voice

in community

in creation

and more

An imprint of InterVarsity Press
Downers Grove, Illinois

InterVarsity Press
P.O. Box 1400, Downers Grove, IL 60515-1426
World Wide Web: www.ivpress.com
E-mail: email@ivpress.com

InterVarsity Press® is the book-publishing division of InterVarsity Christian Fellowship/USA®, a movement of students and faculty active on campus at hundreds of universities, colleges and schools of nursing in the United States of America, and a member movement of the International Fellowship of Evangelical Students. For information about local and regional activities, write Public Relations Dept., InterVarsity Christian Fellowship/USA, 6400 Schroeder Rd., P.O. Box 7895, Madison, WI 53707-7895, or visit the IVCF website at <www.intervarsity.org>.

While all stories in this book are true, some names and identifying information in this book have been changed to protect the privacy of the individuals involved.

Cover design: Cindy Kiple
Cover images: Still life of lemons(front cover and spine): © Allan Jenkins/Trevillion Images
lemon and orange (back cover): © Branko Miokovic/iStockphoto
Interior design: Beth Hagenberg

ISBN 978-0-8308-3821-9

Printed in the United States of America ∞

InterVarsity Press is committed to protecting the environment and to the responsible use of natural resources. As a member of Green Press Initiative we use recycled paper whenever possible. To learn more about the Green Press Initiative, visit <www.greenpressinitiative.org>.

Library of Congress Cataloging-in-Publication Data

Peace, Richard.
Noticing God : in mystical encounters, in the ordinary, in the still small voice, in community, in creation, and more / Richard Peace.
p. cm.
Includes bibliographical references (p.).
ISBN 978-0-8308-3821-9 (pbk. : alk. paper)
1. God (Christianity)—Knowableness. 2. Spirituality. 3. Presence of God. 4. God—Omnipresence. I. Title.
BT102.P35 2012
231.7—dc23

2012005245

P 20 19 18 17 16 15 14 13 12 11 10 9 8 7 6 5 4 3 2 1
Y 28 27 26 25 24 23 22 21 20 19 18 17 16 15 14 13 12

This book is dedicated
to my wonderful grandchildren
who have made life so much richer:

❖

Christopher Tito
Hartley "Jim" Peace Howe
Ezra Peace Howe
Allison Tito

Life is this simple: We are living in a world that is absolutely transparent and God is shining through it all the time. This is not just a fable or a nice story. It is true. If we abandon ourselves to God and forget ourselves, we see it sometimes, and we see it maybe frequently. God manifests Himself everywhere, in everything, in people and in things and in nature and in events. It becomes very obvious that He is everywhere and in everything and we cannot be without Him. You cannot be without God. It's impossible. It's simply impossible.

Thomas Merton

Contents

Introduction

How Do We Notice the Presence of God?

Where is God? How do we notice the presence of God? How do we encounter this God that we sense? How do we know it is God and not some figment of our imagination? Is it possible to know God at all?

Questions like these have interested me for as long as I can remember. I suppose it all started when I was a child, probably around five or six years old, and I had a mystical experience. I call it a "mystical experience" though at the time I did not have the language to name this experience nor any context within which to understand it. My parents were not churchgoers at the time. I had not yet been to Sunday school, so the experience was, as it were, out of the blue.

What happened is this. I was alone in my bedroom in our house in Detroit. I was standing near the back window when I felt a Presence there with me in the room—a Presence that felt big and powerful and overwhelming. I thought it must be God. I was a bit scared being there with that mysterious Presence. I had the sense that this Presence knew me.

This is what I remember now, many years later. I told no one about it at the time. There really was no one to tell. It was only years later, after I had consciously started to follow Jesus, that I talked about this experience.

It was not just that single childhood experience that motivated me to write on this topic. In fact, a whole series of experiences, over time, have fed into these reflections on God-encounters. A key contributor has been my ongoing fascination with and exploration of the phenomenon of conversion.[1] In South Africa, during nearly a decade of ministry there, we saw people "get converted." Sometimes it was sudden, unexpected, even at times undesired, but still the impact was powerful. At other times the conversion process was just that—a process. It took place over time. People just got interested in Jesus, linked up with others who were trying to follow Jesus, and a shift began to take place in their lives. But no matter how conversion happened, people were changed. They started living and thinking in new ways, better ways. Not that they became perfect. Whatever conversion was, it was not a painless path to perfection. But something happened to them and it was good. They said it was "God."

Other God-encounters that took place in my own experience have also motivated me to write, as have the variety of mystical encounters reported throughout history (more on both of these topics will come in the pages ahead). Something is going on. Of course, to have an experience and then attribute it to "God" is not a demonstration that it is actually from God. But the sheer volume of such reports makes them worthy of examination.

All this is set in the context of our current fascination with spirituality. A pervasive conversation is going on in our culture at this point in time about God and about spiritual experience. This conversation makes itself known especially in our films (*The Matrix, The Lord of the Rings, The Tree of Life*), our music

(Bruce Springsteen, U2), and in other cultural artifacts such as painting, sculpture and dance. Something is going on.

THE HABITUAL PRESENCE OF GOD

It is not just that we want to know about God. We want to know God. On the personal level, this longing for the presence of God is described well by Diogenes Allen, the famous Princeton Seminary theologian and philosopher. He writes about his own desire to experience God:

> In spite of my religious faith, the ability to preach sermons and to give lectures that were as good (or bad) as those of the next person, most of the time God seemed remote. Although I had a doctorate in philosophy and theology, and had read a lot of books, I did not know what it meant to have an awareness of God in daily life, or how one went about achieving it. How was it that in all my church attendance and advanced education I had not learned such an elementary matter? . . . [M]y condition would have been easily recognizable by anyone familiar with spiritual theology, a branch of theology that has been neglected in recent times. My condition is called a desire for God's "habitual presence."

He then goes on to say that "by taking part in common religious practices such as going to church, reading the Bible, and praying before meals, sooner or later we feel a vague but persistent urge for something more, an urge that we cannot describe very well." Allen describes how, with guidance, we can learn to satisfy this hunger for more and thus become "increasingly aware of God's presence."[2]

I resonated deeply with this "desire for God's 'habitual presence'" when I first read Dr. Allen's book. He gave me a name for what I too desired. In fact, as I look back on my life and ministry I realize that it was this issue that fascinated me, even if I did not have the categories to describe it. It is one thing to believe in God, as I did. It is quite another to encounter God's presence, which is what I desired (and had experienced from time to time).

How do God-encounters happen? How do we open ourselves to this habitual presence of God? How do we move from believing in God to noticing God in the world around us?

The Discipline of Noticing God

Let me put this another way. I have come to believe that God is present in our world. In fact, God's presence pervades our world. God is not in hiding. The problem is with us. We don't know where to look or what to expect. We do not seem to notice. We need to learn to notice. We need to engage in what I have come to call the "spiritual discipline of noticing God."

While this name is my own creation (as far as I know), it describes a host of practices known by various titles down through the ages. Perhaps the most widely known description is from Brother Lawrence: "practicing the presence of God." Thomas Kelly, the Quaker mystic, calls this "the practice of inward orientation, of inward worship and listening." Klaus Bockmuehl calls this "listening to the God who speaks," and Ben Campbell Johnson speaks of "deepening our sense of the Divine Presence."

I think it is helpful to describe this practice in terms of a spiritual discipline. Spiritual disciplines have been practiced for hundreds of years in the Catholic and Orthodox traditions. In recent years, Protestants have also begun to rediscover spiritual disciplines and to understand that such practices yield valuable spiritual fruit. The spiritual discipline of noticing God underlies many of the other spiritual practices such as meditative prayer (in which we seek to open ourselves to the presence of God), *lectio divina* (hearing God's word to us from Scripture and then responding) and hospitality (treating a stranger as if he or she were Christ). To make this a conscious practice is to build a fundamental reality into daily life: noticing God.

We are meant to be creatures who inhabit two worlds: the natural and the supernatural. But the natural world is so present to us with all its buzzing sights, sounds, tastes and smells that we scarcely notice that other reality—unless we take time to notice. This is what practicing the spiritual discipline of noticing God brings: a sense of the supernatural in the midst of the natural. This gives a wholeness to our living.

I wish it were possible for me to say that I have now mastered this subject and discovered all there is to say about noticing God. In fact, quite the opposite is true. The more I know, the more mysterious the whole question of God-encounters seems to me. That men and women have claimed that they met God in various ways and at various times and places is clear. But the nature of such meetings, which is so difficult to capture in mere language, is still mysterious. Even more mysterious is the question of how to arrange another meeting with God.

Furthermore, I wish I could claim that my own life is filled with the immediate presence of God. I wish it were. I wish I were more faithful in putting myself in those places (such as retreat centers) where God tends to show up if we listen long enough in the silence. I wish I were more regular in engaging in those daily spiritual practices that enable us over time to touch the whisper of God. I wish I were more aware during weekly worship when God seems to be in and amongst all of us. But I can report here what I have come to understand of God-encounters via my reading, my study and my ongoing experience, knowing that what I say is partial and incomplete. All I can hope to do is to be one voice, part of a growing literature on this topic, pointing in the right direction.

One thing I do know with great certainty is that God cannot be boxed in, defined by any formula or summoned by any magic incantation. The prime mover in God-encounters is God. At best all we can do is to put ourselves in those places where we can listen and engage in those practices that enable us to notice God. But mostly it is God.

Core Themes

Noticing God in the midst of life—this is what this book is all about. I want to explore the various ways by which it is possible to meet God in this life. Specifically I want to look at seven different ways in which men and women have come to touch the Living God. I want to look at experiences that range from the dramatic (mystical experiences) to the mundane (hints and intuitions that come to us).

In structuring this book, I begin with dramatic experiences. Chapter one is about noticing God in *mystical encounters.* It turns out that a surprising number of adult Americans have had what can only be described as mystical experiences. But the problem with mystical encounters is that they are unexpected and rare. So in chapter two, in contrast to the God of the exceptional moment, I want to look at noticing *God in the ordinary.* The Jesuits have a lot to teach us about the God of daily life and how to nurture an actual relationship with that God. In chapter three I turn to the related question of noticing God within us—the nature of *the still small voice* by which God, at times, addresses us. What do we do with the hints, whispers, intuitions, dreams and convictions that seem to come from a source other than ourselves? Chapter four explores *the power of community*—noticing God in other people. It is almost a truism that we meet God in others, but what does this really mean? What is the role of spiritual gifts and spiritual fruits when it comes to God-tinged encounters with other people?

Then in chapter five I want to touch on the vast subject of noticing God in *the written Word.* The Bible has been the Christian casebook down through the ages that describes the ongoing interaction of God with this planet. And there is no shortage of people who are willing to tell us that reading those descriptions has changed their lives. Chapter six touches on the challenging question of noticing God in *creation, culture and creativity.* Again, it is an assumption that God is present in creation, but what does this mean? Where do we find God in nature? I also want to consider the related question of noticing God in culture via works of art and the creative process that produces art—both aspects of so-called natural revelation. The seventh chapter is given over to noticing God in *church;* I look at the role of worship in revealing God, in particular the sacraments, as well as at the various aspects of church life such as teaching, spiritual practices and disciplines, service, and retreat in which one encounters God.

Underlying this exploration of avenues by which we encounter God is the question of *discernment:* how do we know that it is God whom we are meeting and not just our fanciful imagination? This is crucial. I have come to believe that we can engage God directly via an "intermittent conversation," to use the most perceptive phrase of Dallas Willard.[3] Our task is to learn to notice God in God's various manifestations and then to respond to the God we meet. Without response there is no transformation. All this will be discussed in the final chapter, "How Do We Know It Is God?"

What I am trying to say in all this is that God is alive, present and accessible in our world today when we know where to look and how to look. But having said this let me repeat that God constantly eludes our categories. God simply will not be put in a box. For example, we cannot guarantee that if we engage in the ancient practice of Bible reading called *lectio divina* that we will automatically meet God (though I will argue that engaging in this practice over time will produce a kind of transformation in us that rings of God). Our task is to learn to notice. And by noticing with discernment over time we gain a sense of God's reality and presence. This is the witness of countless men and women down through the ages.

Core Assumptions

Before we start, you should know the underlying assumptions that I bring to this topic. First, I have come to believe that *God is deeply present in our world.* It is as if our whole world is immersed in a far greater reality—a supernatural world. Think of two spheres with our world as a small sphere resting in the midst of a vast sphere, the presence of which permeates our world. Mostly we are oblivious to that other world, even though we were created to live simultaneously and fully in both the natural (material) world and the supernatural (spiritual) world. The ancient Hebrews got this. The Hebrew word *ruach* can be translated as "wind" or as "spirit." "Hebrew knows no clear distinction between the physical, material world, and a wholly separate 'spiritual' world. The two are inextricably linked," as Gordon Mursell puts it.[4] God is present in our world of sight, sound, taste, touch, movement and cognition. But mostly we don't notice God. What we need to do is to learn how to notice God—which is what this book is all about.

Allied to this is the assumption that God is already deeply involved in the lives of all people whether they recognize it or not.

God is already present. Our challenge is to notice that presence.

I also believe that *we can actually encounter the living God.* God is not only present but knowable. God is not an abstract force or an impersonal entity. God is personal, although the categories by which we speak of persons are far too limited to capture this reality. But because we are made in the image of God, there is a resonance between who God is and who we are. We bear the mark of God in our very personhood, and we were meant to know God.

However, *not everything we label "God" is indeed God.* For example, I am very wary of people who are always saying: "God told me this, God told me that," as if they had a hotline to the divine. I am especially wary when their message from God concerns me or others. On the other hand, I think our reluctance to name anything as having "come from God" is equally unhealthy. The challenge is to discern that which is really God.

The great danger when it comes to "hearing God" is attribution—describing our inner wants or needs as "from God" when they are just wishful thinking or unconscious narcissism. Or we imagine that "God made me do it," when really it was just our misguided judgment that got us into the pickle in the first place. The challenge is to discern God's voice in the midst of all the other voices from our culture, our past, our desires, our family and so on. We can very easily call something "God" that is not God. What horrors have been perpetuated in the name of God: Jonestown, the Crusades, persecution of those not of our faith and so many more. It not enough to want to encounter God. We need discernment.

Furthermore, it is *mostly the presence of God we encounter and not the voice of God we hear.* This is an important distinction. We talk about "hearing God" but this "hearing" has got to be understood in the broadest sense. This usually means touching the presence of God. Very occasionally, in touching this sense of presence, it involves some form of communication.

Another core assumption I have come to believe is that *God (mostly) does not invade our presence.* This statement raises a complex question. On the one hand, God wishes to be known. God created us to know him.[5] But on the other hand, God created us to be fully human, and this means standing on our own two feet. "Okay, God, tell me what to do next," is not how we were created to live. Sure, God wants us to walk in God's way. Apart from anything else, God's way is the way of health, wholeness and love. But we need to choose that way. We are not automatons.

You might even say that God is shy. This is a shyness that comes from not wanting to overwhelm us. The raw presence of God would destroy us, of course. We are not built to encounter such an overwhelming Presence. But what I am calling "shyness" comes from not wanting to make us less than human. God wants us to grow up. God created us to make choices and to own those choices. God wants us to embrace life fully and completely. With God looking over our shoulders all the time, as it were, we would remain children. As the Prioress in Ron Hansen's intriguing novel *Mariette in Ecstasy* says, "God gives us just enough to seek Him, and never enough to fully find him. To do more would inhibit our freedom, and our freedom is very dear to God."[6]

So I need to say up front that I do not believe in a garrulous God. I believe that God can and does speak to us, but this is the exception not the rule. I am suspicious of the chatty, talkative God I read about in some of the contemporary Christian literature. But I do think that God guides us through a variety of hints, intuitions, conversation with others, thoughtful reflection and other indirect input from this God-laden world.

If all this is true and we were meant to know God, why is God so hard to find? This is the core question of the book. One thing is clear to me: the problem is not that God is in hiding. We don't have to engage in any sort of ritual or magical incantation to get God's attention. *God is here, now, closer even than our next breath.* The problem is with us. We need to learn to notice. This is what the spiritual discipline of noticing God is all about.

God puts a longing in our hearts for God. As we respond to that longing so we grow closer to God and to the spiritual world within which we are meant to live. It is like waking up to the world of the Spirit. Our eyes are opened. We begin to see in new ways. Likewise, as we say *no* to that inner sense of God, so it grows distant and harder to discern over time.

Finally, *we meet God in a variety of ways.* Sometimes that meeting is powerful and even overwhelming. Most often the meeting is gentle and quiet, more like a whisper than a tornado. Usually the meeting is intermittent. By this I mean that, in my experience, God is present to us in a quiet, unobtrusive way, in the midst of daily life through encounters with others, via our musings and reflection, in the context of our Christian community in its various aspects, including our own devotional activities such as our Bible reading. When God needs to speak directly, God does so through one of the various avenues I will discuss. But mostly it is a matter of just being present to God.

So come along with me and discover how to notice God.

1

Mystical Encounters

Blaise Pascal was one of those rare geniuses who appear from time to time on our planet. A child prodigy, at age twelve he wrote a treatise on the sounds of vibrating bodies. At age sixteen he published a mathematical paper (on conic sections) so advanced that Descartes at first refused to believe a sixteen-year-old could have been the author. Pascal went on to become not only a seminal mathematician but also an experimental physicist, inventing, among other things, the hydraulic press and the syringe.

If scientific achievements were not enough, Pascal was also famous as a writer. *Pensées* is widely considered a masterpiece of French prose. In addition, he was a philosopher who argued against the rationalism of Descartes (yes, the same Descartes whom he amazed as a teenager). In his famous "wager" Pascal makes the case that a wager for the existence of God is a good one, indeed, one that has the possibility of infinite gain and no loss if it is wrong.

Pascal accomplished all this despite being in almost daily pain from the age of eighteen until his death at thirty-nine.

At age thirty-one, Pascal had a mystical experience that changed his life. He writes:

From about half past ten in the evening until about
half past twelve:
Fire!
God of Abraham, God of Isaac, God of Jacob,
Not of the philosophers and scholars.
Certitude. Certitude. Feeling. Joy. Peace.
God of Jesus Christ.
"Thy God and my God."
Forgetfulness of the world and of everything,
except God. . . .
Joy, joy, joy, tears of joy. . . .
"This is eternal life, That they might know Thee,
the only true God,
And Jesus Christ, whom Thou hast sent."
Jesus Christ.
Jesus Christ.[1]

Pascal attempted to capture in words what had happened to him. He pinned what he wrote inside the lining of his coat and transferred it from coat to coat until the time of his death when it was discovered, by accident, by a servant.

So here it is: a mystical experience—a direct encounter with the living God.

Encountering the Living God

Pascal is not alone in this experience. Countless men and women down through the ages have had similar experiences. A research study by Andrew Greeley and William McCready for the National Opinion Research Center at the University of Chicago determined that fully 35 percent of adult Americans have had what can only be deemed a classic mystical experience.[2] The study also revealed that few of these people talked about their experience with others even though they regarded this as the most valuable or among the most significant experiences they ever had.[3] (They feared they would not be believed.) A follow-up to this original study took place in 2005. This time, one-half of the respondents claimed to have had a life-altering spiritual experience.[4] In yet another study, via in-depth interviews, some 60 percent of the respondents reported that "they have had an experience of the presence of God or a 'patterning' of events in their life that persuades them that they are part of a cosmic design."[5]

What I am talking about is not rare. Accounts of mystical experiences are numerous. Sir Alister Hardy, who was the Linacre Professor of Zoology at Oxford, established what he called the Religious Experience Research Unit to collect and analyze reports of such experiences. He asked for people to send him accounts in which they were influenced "by some Power, whether they call it God or not, which may either appear to be beyond their individual selves or partly, or even entirely, within their being."[6] He received thousands of responses. In his first book he analyzes the first 3,000 such responses.

Before we begin our investigation of the various ways in which God reveals himself through the surprisingly common experience of mystical encounter, we need some background. Describing mystical experiences is highly difficult and seldom satisfactory. The event is so beyond our normal frame of reference, so "other" that we can't find words to say what happened, except in the most general terms. Witness Pascal, the great French essayist, fumbling for words to describe his encounter. In fact, in his famous definition of a mystical experience, William James, the father of American psychology, says that the first characteristic of such experiences is *ineffability* (that is, indescribability). In other words, this is an experience that defies expression. A mystical experience is a state of feeling that is difficult if not impossible to capture by mere words.

The other three characteristics of a mystical experience according to James are (1) its *noetic* quality: it brings profound insight; (2) its *transience:* such experiences do not last long; and (3) its *passivity:* the experience comes upon one—"the mystic feels as if his own will were in abeyance, and indeed sometimes as if he were grasped and held by a superior power."[7]

So when exploring mystical experiences we must begin with the knowledge that we will struggle as we seek to grasp their exact nature.

Another important fact about mystical experiences is that they come in a variety of sizes, shapes and forms ranging from the dramatic to the mundane. In fact, this is how I want to treat the topic, by exploring this variety of mystical experiences.

Dramatic Encounters

Sometimes God bursts in on our lives in such a way that even the most insensitive among us cannot miss God's presence. Take St. Paul, for example. A mystical experience was the last thing he was expecting on route to Damascus to search out renegade Jews who had started to follow Jesus. An encounter with Jesus in a mystical vision was probably Paul's worst nightmare. And yet this is just what he says happened.

It was midday. Suddenly there was a powerful light, brighter even than the blazing middle-eastern sun—a light that had such force that it threw Paul and his companions to the ground. (Notice that this "force" impacted the whole group and not just Paul.) In the midst of that light Paul hears a voice: "Saul, Saul, why are you persecuting me?" This is no anonymous numinous force but a person who knew Saul's language and Saul's name (Saul was Paul's pre-Christian name). Furthermore, this particular question turns out to be the exact question that unlocks for Paul the meaning of his life. By it he comes to realize what he had really been doing. Saul/Paul thought he was upholding God's law by participating in the apprehension, jailing and at times execution of Christians, but it turns out that he was on the wrong side of this issue. He had been persecuting not just Christians but the mysterious "me" who addresses him. Incidentally, he was also breaking the sixth commandment against killing.

But who is this person in the midst of the vision? Paul asks: "Who are you, Lord?" to which the answer comes: "I am Jesus of Nazareth, whom you are persecuting." Not the answer he wanted!

The long and the short of all this is that Saul the zealous Pharisee turned almost instantly into Paul the Christian apostle. There is no other way under heaven or earth by which this could have happened to a man like Paul apart from a direct encounter with the resurrected Jesus in a mystical experience.

Perhaps Paul's experience is atypical, but it is far from unique. The literature of Christian spirituality is replete with such experiences. In fact, I was teaching a new course in Christian spirituality at Fuller Theological Seminary in which I examined the lives of eight spiritual pioneers from the contemplative tradition: Patrick of Ireland, Benedict of Nursia, Hildegard of Bingen, Francis of Assisi, Clare of Assisi, Julian of Norwich, Ignatius of Loyola and Francis de Sales. As I was putting the course together, it occurred to me that all eight of these people had one or more mystical encounters that changed their lives and shaped their ministries.

Patrick, while a slave in Ireland, had a dream in which he heard God telling him that a ship was waiting to take him home. He got up and walked some two hundred miles to a place he had never been, avoiding detection as an escaped slave, and found a ship back to Europe. Benedict had a vision in which he saw the entire world "as if gathered into a single ray of light," "seeing as God sees," as one of his biographers put it. Hildegard had numerous visions that she expressed via music and in her paintings. In a vision Francis received stigmata (the wounds of the crucified Jesus). His friend and colleague Clare had to be reminded to eat, so deeply did she sink into her visions. In a vision, Ignatius met the Jesus whom he sought to follow his whole life. (He had started the Society of Jesus, better known as the Jesuits.) Early in his life, Francis de Sales had come to feel that he was not one of those "chosen" by God so at death he would go to hell. He prayed to God, asking that despite the fact that he was dammed, he could be allowed to serve God in this life (as a priest) since he would be unable to serve God in the hereafter. One day while praying in a church in Paris, Francis heard a voice say to him: "I do not call myself the Damning One, my name is Jesus." His fears vanished and his life was changed.

And then there is Julian of Norwich. On May 8, 1373, she had a sixteen-part mystical vision that lasted twenty-four hours. She describes this vision in great detail in *Revelations of Divine Love* (and in so doing became the first woman in history to write a book in English). Julian pondered these visions for the next twenty years, seeking to understand what God was telling her, knowing that these visions were not just for her but also for others. She then penned a second, longer description of her mystical experience, which is a highly sophisticated theological reflection on God that influenced people as diverse as C. S. Lewis, T. S. Eliot and Bishop Desmond Tutu.

Mystical experiences are potent stuff.

Brushes with the Divine

But not all encounters with the numinous are big, dramatic and overpowering. In fact, I have come to feel that most God-encounters are mild, almost glancing. It is as if we brush up against the Divine and life shines brighter for a moment.

For example, I was sitting in the back garden of the Franciscan monastery in Santa Barbara, California. It was a lovely summer day, warm with a gentle breeze. Birds were chirping. The silence was intense and inviting. And for a moment I had a fleeting sense of Presence. It was as if this place, rich with the prayers of countless people over time, was imbued with a sense of the Divine. This was a holy place where "the membrane between heaven and earth was thin" (as St. Columba, a sixth-century Irish monk, put it).

N. T. Wright, the former Anglican bishop of Durham, tells about visiting a building in Montreal that had once been a United Church of Canada. Now decommissioned, it had been turned into a concert hall.

> The first time we went there, to a very "secular" occasion, I was stunned. I walked in and sensed the presence of God, gentle but very strong. I sat through the loud concert wondering if I was the only person who felt it, and reflecting on the fact that I had no theology by which to explain why a redundant United church should feel that way. The only answer I have to this day is that when God is known, sought and wrestled with in a place, a memory of that remains.[8]

The challenge is to be alert to such "touches." They come on us unawares, often in odd places and at odd times. I find that such experiences often occur in places of great natural beauty, where God's creative handiwork seems to blossom around us. Perhaps this is just because in such places I am more apt to notice what is happening there. In fact, this touch of the Divine seems to come at those times when life shifts out of the normal for a moment: when we are in pain or we experience great pleasure, when we are listening to music that makes us catch our breath or we are viewing great art that touches our souls. There is such an array of these kinds of moments: canoeing at dawn on a New Hampshire lake; standing in front of the great cathedral in Orvieto, Italy, in the late afternoon when the sun makes the façade sparkle and come alive; singing "The Church's One Foundation" with a vast congregation caught up in this great hymn; catching a glimpse off to one side of something familiar that for a moment becomes new. The world is, indeed, alive with God.

Longings and God

C. S. Lewis provides an interesting perspective on mystical experiences when he talks about what he calls "the inconsolable longing." With this phrase Lewis has in mind those moments when, for an instance, we are drawn away from this world into another world—a hidden world in which we find ourselves deeply at home. This sense is triggered by various inputs: a line of poetry, a childhood memory, a snatch of conversation, an image that resonates deeply. But just as quickly as this sense of that other world comes upon us it vanishes, leaving behind a deep longing for whatever it was we encountered. We may return to the music or the words or the place that triggered the experience, but we find there only the longing. Lewis would argue that these are genuine intimations that our true home is with God, and that someday, God willing, we will live there.

Lewis himself is the one who best describes this sort of mystical insight. In a sermon titled "The Weight of Glory" (first given at the Oxford University Church in the midst of World War II) he gives voice to this inconsolable longing:

> Our lifelong nostalgia, our longing to be reunited with something in the universe from which we now feel cut off, to be on the inside of some door which we have always seen from the outside, is no mere neurotic fancy, but the truest index of our real situation. . . . Do what they will, then, we remain conscious of a desire which no natural happiness will satisfy. But is there any reason to suppose that reality offers any satisfaction to it? . . . A man's physical hunger does not prove that that man will get any bread; he may die of starvation on a raft in the Atlantic. But surely a man's hunger does prove that he comes from a race which repairs its body by eating and inhabits a world where eatable substance exists. In the same way, though I do not believe (I wish I did) that my desire for Paradise proves that I shall enjoy it, I think it a pretty good indication that such a thing exists and that some men will.[9]

In *Mere Christianity* Lewis adds this explanatory comment: "If I find in myself a desire which no experience in this world can satisfy, the most probable explanation is that I was made for another world."[10] This "inconsolable longing" is all about touching for a moment that other world, that bigger reality within which our reality rests. Such a touch can be unnerving and deeply moving.

I have come to feel that this sense of "inconsolable longing" is an intensified form of what I have called "brushes with God," which are a gentle feeling that remains with us for a while. In contrast, the inconsolable longing is often sharp, intense, immediate and fleeting. It is a pang of desire, a bolt of insight, and it is often painful in a good sort of way. By it we catch a glimpse of who we are, where our true home is and thus where we belong. And we find that we deeply desire to be part of that destiny. But then the window closes on this vision and all we are left with is the longing. Surely this is a deep truth about actual reality.

Brain Research and God

But are such experiences anything more than brain blips, generated by our internal chemistry and wiring? In recent years, due in large part to the development of new scanning devices, we know a great deal more about how the brain functions. In fact, it is now possible to watch various parts of the brain light up during religious practices such as meditating, praying in tongues or engaging in intercessory prayer. It is also possible to discern certain markers in the brain left behind by spiritual events.

Scientists are busy exploring the physiology of spiritual experience. A fascinating account of this research appears in *Fingerprints of God: The Search for the Science of Spirituality*, a book by Barbara Bradley Hagerty, National Public Radio's award-winning religious correspondent, in which she relates her conversations with a number of the scientists conducting this research.

What do these studies show? Well, scientists have found, for example, that during meditation the frontal lobes of nuns and monks light up,[11] while their parietal lobes go dark when they are in deep prayer.[12] Research also indicates that meditation, over time, changes the structure of the brain.[13] Scientists now know a lot more about the biology of mystical experience as well. It seems that "the serotonin system may serve as a biological basis for spiritual experiences."[14] Also, a hormone called oxytocin can bring on an "oceanic" feeling associated with mystical experiences,[15] and the very chemistry of our brain makes it possible to see visions.[16] I am not sure of what all this means, but it does signify, as Hagerty details, that the whole question of spiritual experience is becoming a lively topic within the scientific community.

What does all this research say about the origin of mystical experiences? Are they from God or merely generated by the brain? The answer to this question, on one level, depends on the paradigm by which one approaches the data. A materialistic worldview has no room for God; a spiritual worldview allows for the possibility of God. Thus, Freud (a thorough-going materialist) felt that God was an illusion and spiritual experience could be explained away (it was nothing but a form of delusional thinking); while his colleague Jung (with a worldview that allowed for the spiritual) developed a paradigm of human personality that put God (and God-encounters) at the foundation of personality.

Hagerty concludes that spiritual experiences leave a "residue in one's brain or body." She continues:

> Science is showing that spiritual experience leaves fingerprints, evidence that a spiritual transaction has occurred. . . . Simply put, when you bump against the spiritual, something changes. First, your brain begins to operate differently, even at resting state. Second, your interior life is transformed. Your priorities and loves, how you choose to spend your time and with whom you choose to spend it—all that changes in a blink of an eye.[17]

What all this says to me about mystical experiences is this: mystical experiences are *experiences,* and all human experience, by necessity, is processed by the human brain. We need a way to apprehend what happens to us and in us—a subjective perception that enables us to encounter mystical reality. We could not have a mystical experience unless we had the ability to apprehend that experience, and this is what the brain does for us. As one researcher put it, "we are neurologically equipped to be able to connect with God."[18] In other words, *the brain has the inherent capability for mystical experience.* It could be no other way. So when certain sections of the cerebral cortex light up when one is meditating, this is the mechanism by which we process that experience in real time. It is quite remarkable, I have come to believe, that God has created human beings in such a way that we have the capability of experiencing God. We are not locked into a space/time world with no way out. We have the ability to experience the spiritual realm. This is a wonderful and remarkable gift.

SIGNIFICANCE

So what does all this mean? It is clear that men and women down through the ages have felt that they have encountered one who is Wholly Other. What is the significance of this fact?

First, such seminal events give witness to the fact that God is present and knowable, that our deep desire to encounter the Divine can be realized, and that we can learn to notice God in the world around us. This affirms that our search for spiritual enlightenment is not futile. There is a God who is still speaking. We are thus motivated to carry on. This reality propels us on our spiritual quest.

Second, the range and variety of mystical experiences should invite us to search our past and ask, Have I had a mystical experience of some sort and failed to recognize it as such? Then we can ask, In such experiences, what was there for me to know and do? What did these teach me about God? What was God calling me to be?

Third, the fact of mystical experiences reveals to us that we do not live in a closed universe. Christians have long known that we are meant to live in two worlds: the material and the spiritual. So mystical experiences call us to that other reality. They remind us that to be undivided human beings we need to open ourselves to the Divine. Therein lies our wholeness.

Fourth, some men and women in our culture, both past and present, seem especially attuned to the mystical. We call them, not surprisingly, mystics. Some of these mystics have written about their experiences and we can learn from their encounters. Of course, as with other subjective accounts, we need to be cautious as we read this literature. People can (and do) claim all sorts of wild things that are by their very nature beyond scrutiny. Just because a mystic claims something does not make it true. On the other hand, some of these spiritual voyagers have profound insights into God. Julian of Norwich is one such person who deserves careful reading. It is wise to stay away from fringe voices of an esoteric nature and listen to those whose voices have an authenticity verified by many witnesses down through the ages. Furthermore, we listen to those in whose lives the fruit of love validates their experiences.

In all this we need to remember the perspective of the mystics. They give witness to the fact that such encounters, while meaningful, are not the purpose of life. Mystical experiences enrich us. They propel us into the future with a deep sense of hope. They give us confidence. But they are not the stuff of daily life. Mother Teresa wrote to her archbishop (who was not much interested in "voices and visions") about her own mystical experiences: "They came unasked—and they have gone. They have not changed my life. They have helped me to be more trustful and draw closer to God. . . . Why they came I do not know—neither do I try to know. I am pleased to let Him do with me just as it pleaseth Him."[19]

Finally, since we cannot "order up" a mystical experience, it is not healthy to become preoccupied with having such an encounter. I have known people who are preoccupied with mystical encounters. They seem to spend their lives running after every new (seeming) manifestation of the power of God. So they only attend churches that promise spectacle and power. They travel to places such as Toronto to experience the so-called Toronto Blessing or to Mozambique where it is said that the dead have been raised. They are spiritual vagabonds always seeking to be in on the next great thing God is said to be doing and not spiritual pilgrims (as we are called to be) alert to what God is doing in ordinary life. If God-encounters happen, they happen by God's grace and for God's purposes. In the meantime, we need to learn to notice the presence of God in everyday life, the subject of the next chapter.

2

God in the Ordinary

I, for one, am glad that God reveals himself directly to us in our space/time reality via mystical experiences. A God who is just an intellectual construct would be suspect. On the other hand, it would be just as problematic if God were only found in the wonder of mystical encounter. A God who comes only on occasion (maybe once or twice in a lifetime), and then dramatically, is a God of the exceptional moment.

We need a God of everyday life, a God who is nearer to us than our next breath, one whose love surrounds us as we go about ordinary life. In fact, this is how the Bible describes God—as one who is present in our space/time reality.[1] The challenge of course, is to apprehend the presence of God in the midst of our busy world. This is the question I consider in this chapter: How do we come to know God in daily life?

Meet Saint Ignatius

Here I have found the insights of St. Ignatius of Loyola to be profound. He wrestled with this very question in his spiritual pilgrimage. Over time he developed what he called the *spiritual exercises,* which had the purpose of enabling us to develop a relationship with God through an ongoing encounter with

Jesus. We can see the power of these exercises in the movement that Ignatius birthed: the Society of Jesus, better known to us as the Jesuits. The Jesuits have had a profound effect on the world around them.

Consider the fact that at one point in history the Jesuits built the world's largest higher-education system, providing a classical education to nearly 20 percent of all Europeans. Currently there are twenty-eight Jesuit-founded colleges operating in the United States including highly regarded universities such as Georgetown, Holy Cross and Boston College. The Jesuits were confidants to rulers in Europe, China, Japan and India. They were explorers, scientists and geographers of note and much more. Not that the Jesuits always got it right or were always on the right side of things. They were notorious for involving themselves (meddling?) in affairs of state. They were even disbanded by the pope for a time in the eighteenth century. (Whether this was justified is another story.) Still, the Jesuits are currently the world's largest religious order with some 21,000 members who run 2,000 institutions in over 100 countries. As someone put it: they are a 450-year-old corporation that is still vigorous, growing and innovative. How did they do this?[2]

The answer is: they learned how to live in the presence of God in the midst of daily life. At the heart of Ignatian spirituality is the principle of "finding God in all things." Jesuits understand that God is involved in every dimension of life: work, family, politics, illness, money, sexuality, music, friendship, culture. You name it, God is there. The challenge, of course, is to find God in all things, but this is what Ignatian spiritual practices are all about: seeing God in the ordinary.

If ever there was an unlikely candidate to begin a new religious order, Ignatius was it.[3] In fact, he would have been at the bottom of the list when it came to people most likely to develop a world-changing religious order. He was born in a castle in the Basque area of Spain in the sixteenth century, the son of minor but well-connected nobility. Growing up he was little interested in education. Rather his mind was filled with the idea of knights and chivalry and courtly love. He was a wildly romantic young man who at age fifteen was sent off to the house of the chief treasurer of Spain to prepare for a life at court. This suited him just fine. He was far more interested in fencing than learning Latin. (As payback for his inattention to his schooling, when he woke up to the need for an education at age thirty-three, he had to sit in a classroom of kids in order to learn Latin!) Ignatius was a bit of a troublemaker, much given to gambling, dueling and involvement with women. He was arrested on at least two occasions for his bad behavior, once when he set off with sword drawn after two people who bumped him in a narrow alley.

How did a guy like this come to know God in such a deep and powerful way that he unleashed a host of Jesus-followers who wanted to change the world for good? This is a complex and involved question, but the short answer is that Ignatius was drawn almost by accident into a compelling relationship with Jesus who became his daily companion. Ignatius learned to know Jesus, to trust Jesus, to follow Jesus and to listen to Jesus. He explains how one can do this in his *Spiritual Exercises*, in which he invites others into the same living relationship with Jesus.

Meeting Up with the Jesuits

I first came into contact with Ignatian spirituality almost by accident. At the time I was a professor at Gordon-Conwell Theological Seminary (in the Boston area). One of my research interests was focused on how people grew in relationship to Jesus (discipleship). Over time I had written a fair amount of material designed to promote growth in discipleship. But the more I read, the more I came to realize there was a whole tradition of spiritual formation (contemplative spirituality) about which Protestants knew little.[4]

At the heart of spiritual formation were the so-called *spiritual disciplines*. These were practices that helped shape our spiritual lives in positive ways. Dallas Willard divides these practices into two categories: disciplines of engagement (such as study, prayer, Bible reading, service and confession) and disciplines of abstinence (such as solitude, silence, fasting and frugality). It seemed to me that these practices could be taken from the monastic environment that had birthed them and adapted to a lay environment and the busy schedules of those engaged with families and jobs.[5]

One of the disciplines that especially caught my attention was spiritual direction. To have a spiritual director seemed to be a good thing, but where did people find a spiritual director? It turned out that there was a Jesuit retreat center a half-hour away from where I lived (Eastern Point Retreat House in Gloucester, Massachusetts). With great hesitation, having put off contacting them for months, I eventually phoned and asked if I could see someone.

It was my great good fortune to be connected with Father John Kerdiejus, S.J. Father John had been a missionary in Jamaica and had recently been assigned to Eastern Point. Father John was older, he was an experienced director, and most importantly, he was a Jesuit with all that this implies, namely, that he had a vital relationship with Jesus and that he was very bright, very well trained and very open to others. Still this was a bit of a stretch for him: to have as a directee a Protestant who was an ordained United Church of Christ minister and a professor at a Protestant theological seminary.

My interest in spiritual direction was not merely academic; it was also personal. I wanted to move deeper into my own spiritual life. I wanted to grow more as a person. to become more self-aware and more loving toward others. What I needed was the kind of relationship with Jesus that made sense in the ordinariness of daily life. As it turned out, Father John and I hit it off immediately, and this led to a decade-long relationship that helped change my life.

The Prayer of Examen

The spiritual practice that enabled me to begin to find God in the midst of ordinary life was the prayer of examen. Noticing God during peak moments of unusual enlightenment is not much of a challenge. But finding God's presence in daily events is much more difficult. Over time I came to realize that it is all about noticing. This is what I eventually came to call the *spiritual discipline of noticing*. The examen proved to be a great way to begin noticing God.

Ignatius called this type of prayer the "examination of conscience." He felt that it was so important that even if his Jesuit brothers were unable to engage in any other form of prayer, they were not to neglect this form of prayer. Ignatius understood that a mission-oriented community such as the Jesuits, who were not tied to church or monastery, and who were often on the move, could not always participate in formal prayer. But, he said, they must never neglect the prayer of examen. It lies at the very heart of Ignatian spiritual practices.

The prayer of examen is all about recollection: specifically, noticing what has been going on in your life during the previous day. In its original form, the prayer of examen had five steps, but the version to which Fr. Kerdiejus introduced me consists of three steps.[6]

Step one involves gratitude. In your mind, go back over the previous twenty-four hours and notice all the gifts God has given you and be grateful. What "benefits" have you been given, to use Ignatius's term? By this he means any good thing you have been given, from good news to a beautiful day, from a fun time with your grandchild to the chance to help out a friend. Recall them, relish them, savor them and enjoy them. And express your gratitude to God. Even on a really bad day we can be grateful for ordinary things such as waking up in the morning or having food to eat that day. There is always something for which we can be grateful. An added benefit of this first step is that over time we have the potential to become grateful people. Gratitude is infectious and a gift to others.

Step two involves awareness of God. Go back over the same twenty-four-hour time period and this time look for the presence of God in your life. Recall the thoughts, words and deeds of the day. Where was God in all of this? Where was there love, joy or peace in your life? What made you happy? Sad? Stressed? Confused? How was God with you in the hard times or in the joyous moments? Did you experience the presence of God in other people? At first this kind of examination may be difficult simply because we have not learned to notice the ways in which God connects to our daily life. But over time, we develop the ability to see. When we do, we live differently because we notice the ongoing presence of God. It is as if an inner weight is lifted from how we engage in life when we know that God is with us in it.

I should note, however, that sometimes it is very hard to find God in our lives. And in praying the examen we may be reduced to saying: "I know you were there but I don't know where." This is okay.

Step three involves confession. For the third time, reflect on the previous twenty-four hours. This time look for those instances in which you slipped up, did it wrong, did it for the wrong reasons, did the wrong, said *no* to a chance to reach out or in some way failed to be who God calls you to be. This is the confession/repentance part of the prayer. As human beings we are meant to grow, to become all we are called to be. But we fail along the way by "sins of commission" (doing what is wrong) and "sins of omission" (failing to do what is right). Jesus offers forgiveness when we fail. We grow when we own that failure and deal with it. And the prayer of examen gives us an avenue by which to note, name and confess. The interesting thing about confession in the context of God's gifts and presence is that the sting is far less. We know that we are confessing to a loving, giving God who knows our names. This makes all the difference.

The prayer of examen works well for me. I can use it as I drive to work in the morning on Southern California's notorious freeways. It gives me a chance to remember and review the previous day—what happened, what it was like, what I learned (or needed to learn). I become more conscious. This is crucial.

Spiritual formation is all about becoming more conscious, noticing what is happening in you and around you and saying *yes* to this and *no* to that. You do this "review of the day" from the standpoint of gratitude—gratitude to God for the concrete gifts of life in the previous twenty-four hours. For me this perspective is important. I am not, by nature, a person filled with gratitude. I tend to worry. But over time, this attitude of gratitude is helping me become a more trusting and joyful person—and this makes me grateful. The prayer of examen also forces me to notice the Divine Presence in its various (and often subtle) manifestations. It helps me be present to the Presence. For me this awareness has become key to being open to world of the Spirit in the midst of the materialistic world.

Finally, via the prayer of examen I get to ponder what I have done or have not done. I get to reflect on how I need to change—often in small but important ways. So when my wife comments on something I have said or done and my initial response is defensive, the next day I get to come back to the incident in a more open frame of mind. The prayer of examen keeps me present to myself, to the world around me, to the world of the Spirit and to God. I need that. Thank you, St. Ignatius.

Ignatian Contemplation

A second spiritual practice opens up for us the reality of Jesus. This is Ignatian contemplation, also called imaginative prayer. It too is quite simple and very powerful. Basically, this involves imagining that we are present in one of the Gospel stories. In our imagination we enter into the story. We participate in the events. We open ourselves to Jesus in the story and we let happen what happens. In other words, we invite God to speak to us via our imagination.

Ignatius is big on imagination—because this is how he came to faith in the first place. How he got converted is an interesting story. When he was a young man, Ignatius was involved in a border skirmish between the Spanish and the French. Although they were greatly outnumbered, Ignatius rallied his Spanish troops to charge the French. (Remember that he was a highly romantic and rather foolish young man.) In the course of this charge Ignatius got wounded in the leg. After the battle the French surgeons set his leg but they did not do a very good job so when it healed he limped. Being rather vain, Ignatius insisted that the leg be rebroken and reset properly so he would not limp (all this in the days before anesthesia). He could not imagine life at the court if he limped.

During the long months of recuperation at the family castle

in Loyola, Ignatius got bored. He asked for something to read. Not much was available, but his brother's wife brought him two books. One was on the lives of the saints and the other on the life of Jesus. As he read these stories he would let his mind wander and imagine what it would be like to live as a saint or walk with Jesus. He noticed an interesting thing. Unlike his imagining that he did great deeds as a knight for his king and his lady, which left him flat afterwards, this new imagining brought joy and peace. Over time he actually came to desire to live like a saint following Jesus.

So it was not surprising that Ignatius used his imagination in prayer. He did not invent imaginative prayer, but he popularized it and made it part of his spiritual exercises.

Here is the process.

Step one is to read over a story from the life of Jesus. Read it carefully. Read it a number of times. Study it. Read what others have written about this particular story. In other words, try to develop a good grasp of the story before you seek to make it the focus of your prayer.

Step two is to imagine yourself in the midst of the story. Get quiet. Get still. Close your eyes. Imagine you are at the scene of the story. Begin by paying attention to the setting. What do you see? Notice the details of the place. What does it feel like to be there? What do you smell? Taste? Now what do you hear? What is going on around you? In other words, enter the story with all your senses alert.

Once you have a good feel for the place, *step three is to watch events unfold with you as part of the drama.* Sink into the scene. Relax in the presence of this unfolding event. Listen to what Jesus is saying. Engage Jesus in conversation. You have no script beyond the story in its original form. Just go with the flow with no expectations, no judgments, no needs except to pay attention.

Finally, after a time, come up out of the meditation and *begin to write in your journal.* Try to capture what happened. What was said? What was said to you? Move beyond the events to your feelings: What did you feel? Why? What does all this mean in the context of your life? What new insights do you have?

You will be surprised at what you discover when you give yourself to this form of prayer.

Experiencing the Baptism of Jesus

Let me illustrate the process, albeit in abbreviated form. Suppose that the story you choose is Mark 1:4-11, the baptism of Jesus. This is a powerful story, filled with detail and mystery, so it is a good one to use as the basis for your prayer. Begin with study. As you explore the passage, pay attention to John the Baptist. Who is he? What role does he play in history? What does he look like according to this passage? What was the purpose of baptism in the first century? These are just some of the study questions that will drive you deeper into the text. It is often good to study the text the day before you engage in this form of prayer. It allows the material to sink in. It also lets you ponder the passage longer before you try praying it.

When you decide to enter imaginatively into the story, begin with a relaxation exercise. Then in a quiet state with eyes closed, imagine that you are at the River Jordan. Notice all the people who are there, young and old, rich and poor, all eager, all expectant. Smell the water and dust mixing together. Feel the hot sun beating down on the crowd. Pay special attention to John, who is a very odd man, dressed like an Old Testament prophet with fire in his eyes and conviction in his voice. Listen to him address the people, telling them about the Coming One. Watch him baptize the people. Let him baptize you. Feel the water as you step into it and walk toward John. Let John take you down under the water and then bring you back up. Return to the riverbank. Now watch Jesus and his disciples arrive. Pay close attention to all that goes on in the baptism of Jesus. And so on . . .

Now I know that this sounds a lot like "making things up" and imagining that Jesus is speaking to us. While we are quite capable of self-deception, in fact this type of meditation can be a powerful form of prayer. When we are listening carefully, God can and does communicate with us. Of course, you won't be convinced of this just by my saying it. You need to try it for yourself. I believe that when we pray this way, by means of the God-given gift of imagination, we are reaching out to God and God is reaching out to us. So interesting things happen. Is it Jesus who is actually talking to us in our imagination? I am not comfortable claiming this. But I do know from experience that we get all sorts of new insights when engaged in Ignatian contemplation. "The Jesus in my imagination" often says quite unexpected things that make me stop, listen and ponder.

The Spiritual Exercises

The prayer of examen and Ignatian contemplation are found in the *Spiritual Exercises* of St. Ignatius. Ignatius worked on the *Spiritual Exercises* for over twenty-five years (between 1522 and 1548). The book consists of a set of guidelines for spiritual directors whose job it is to walk with individuals through a very focused thirty-day retreat. The Spiritual Exercises retreat is an extended meditation on the life of Jesus—which makes sense given that Jesus is at the very heart of Jesuit spirituality (the Society of Jesus). The purpose of this thirty-day retreat is to come to know Jesus in a new and deeper way and in so doing to find freedom to become all you are meant to be, to experience the love of God and to make good decisions about the life God is calling you to lead.

Ignatius's *Spiritual Exercises* is not a book that you can pick up and read easily. I tried to read the *Spiritual Exercises* off and on for years, never making much headway. People said it was a spiritual classic, but I found it to be a spiritual mystery until I figured out that it was not meant to be read, it was meant to be experienced.[7] The retreat director is the one who reads it as he guides others in the experience. Eventually I got to do an eight-day Ignatian retreat, and the exercises came alive for me.

It is by means of the spiritual exercises that Jesuits are shaped for ministry (and for life). Out of this thirty-day retreat they become far more self-aware (and learn to stay aware); they encounter Jesus who becomes a reality to them (and whose disciples they become); and they consciously say *yes* to the invitation to enter a life of ministry with the Society of Jesus. As James Martin, S.J., puts it: "The way of Ignatius is about finding freedom: the freedom to become the person you're meant to be, to love and to accept love, to make good decisions, and to experience the beauty of creation and the mystery of God's love."[8]

But it is not just Jesuits who benefit by engaging in the spiritual exercises. They are accessible to everyone, and these days they are offered in various formats, including at weekend retreats, via spiritual direction and in small group formats. At Fuller Theological Seminary we have offered from time to time a nine-month version (based on the work of Joseph Tetlow, S.J.) that consists of one hour per day in prayer and meditation, one hour per week meeting with a directed small group, and one hour per month meeting with a spiritual director. No matter what form these groups might take, they help make Jesus more real to us on a daily basis and they teach us to notice the work of God in our lives.

Meeting Jesus

I am sure you have noticed the shift in focus in this chapter. In chapter one I focused on God (of the mystical encounter). But here in chapter two I have focused on Jesus (of daily life). In the later chapters I will focus on the Holy Spirit (of inner experience). This shift in focus is intentional. In Christian spirituality we talk about God the Father, God the Son and God the Holy Spirit: Creator, Redeemer and Sustainer. Or as the third-century North African theologian Tertullian put it in his wonderful metaphor by which to understand the Trinity: if God the Father is like the sun, then Jesus is a sunbeam of the same substance directed to earth, and the Holy Spirit is the spot of warmth and light as the sunbeam arrives on earth. The Holy Spirit is the effect.[9] It is important to talk about each of these emphases since people encounter God in such different ways.

For some, the first encounter is with God the Creator, whom they come to know through a mystical experience or via the wonder of the created world. Others first come to know God the Son. Jesus is what God looks like in human form. Whereas the God of all creation can be remote and frightening, Jesus, who was "one of us," is more accessible. Still others first come to know God the Holy Spirit through such an experience as healing prayer or through spiritual fruits such as love, joy or peace that are manifest in individuals and communities.

No matter where one begins, along the way we encounter God (who is One) in each of these manifestations.

Significance

So what does all this mean? First, men and women have claimed to have an actual relationship with Jesus that helps them grow as individuals. The Jesuits are a great example of what can happen in society when a group of individuals give themselves over to such a relationship with Jesus. Not that the Jesuits are perfect—no group is—but at their best they show what a powerful impact for good a group who seek to follow Jesus (often at great personal cost) can have. Ignatius himself exemplifies the kind of transformation an encounter with Jesus/God can have. If he can be transformed into a great spiritual leader, anyone can!

Second, spiritual practices open us up to the Divine Presence, whether perceived as God, imagined as Jesus or experienced as the power of the Spirit. The prayer of examen helps us notice God in the midst of daily life. Ignatian contemplation enables us, by the use of our imaginations, to connect with the call of Jesus on our lives. And the spiritual exercises put us in touch with the transforming power of God. Of course we only know all this by engaging in these practices.

Finally, a God of the dramatic is one thing. A God of the ordinary is another. We need both. One of the great claims of Christianity is that God is manifest in Jesus. Ordinary life has never been the same since Jesus showed us that the world of matter is sacred.

3

The Still Small Voice

To talk about "having a relationship with Jesus" raises all sorts of questions, not the least of which concerns the nature of that "relationship." What does it mean to "have a relationship with Jesus"? Of necessity such a relationship is interior. Jesus is not physically present any longer. St. Paul recognizes this and talks about "Christ in us," but what does he mean?

As a way into this question of "relationship," this chapter explores what has come to be known as "the still small voice." If we have an interior relationship with God, at the heart of this will be communication. The phrase "still small voice" is one way to talk about such communication. The phrase comes from 1 Kings 19:11-13:

> And behold, the LORD passed by, and a great and strong wind rent the mountains, and broke in pieces the rocks before the LORD, but the LORD was not in the wind; and after the wind an earthquake, but the LORD was not in the earthquake; and after the earthquake a fire, but the LORD was not in the fire; and after the fire *a still small voice.* And when Elijah heard it, he wrapped his face in his mantle and went out and stood at the entrance of the cave. And

> behold, there came a voice to him, and said, "What are you doing here, Elijah?" (RSV; italics added)

Elijah, the Old Testament prophet, has a mystical experience out of which he receives a call from God. (You need to read 1 Kings 19 to get the whole story.) But what interests me is that Elijah's experience combines the coming of God both via a mystical experience filled with power (wind, earthquake, fire) and via an interior experience (a still small voice). The two experiences are, in this case, integrated.

Curiously, the Hebrew word rendered in this translation as a "still small voice" is notoriously difficult to translate. The traditional translation, which the Revised Standard Version of the Bible retains in the quotation above, is changed in the New Revised Standard Version to "a sound of sheer silence," which I rather like. The New International Version translates the word as "a gentle whisper," while the New Jerusalem version has "the sound of a gentle breeze." The New English Bible translates it as "a low murmuring sound." What is going on here? Quite simply, no one really knows what this particular word actually means, though the sense of it is some sort of interior communication.

Dallas Willard, who is a professor of philosophy at the University of Southern California, has a helpful way of describing what is taking place here. He says that the way God addresses us "tak[es] the form of thoughts that are our thoughts, though tangibly not *from* us."[1] Willard goes on to say that "the 'still small voice'—or the 'interior' voice as it also is sometimes called—is the preferred or highest form of individualized communication for God's purposes."[2]

The vagueness of the word is as it should be, for who truly knows the sound of God's inner whisper? The challenge is to learn to recognize that inner voice, over against other inner voices.

Hints, Whispers and Other Intuitions

How does the still small voice differ from the kinds of hints and intuitions that we all get from time to time? You know what I'm talking about. You are driving down the road and you have a sense that you need to take the next right turn. You do so, not knowing why, but a short time later you find yourself at your destination. Or you are having a conversation and you get the sense that although the words are innocuous enough, something else is going on with your conversation partner, something very serious indeed.

What is happening here? Where do these hunches or intuitions come from? Are these from God? Perhaps, but I suspect that most of the time these insights are a product of our unconscious putting together diverse bits of data from various sources. Finding the correct turn may be a matter of having driven this way in years past but forgetting about it on a conscious level. The sense of unease in the conversation may be a matter of unconsciously processing facial clues, the cadence of voice, the eyes of the other, odd words—all the apparatus of nonverbal communication.

I think that our unconscious mind is a far more complex, wonderful and mysterious reality than we know. Here is an example of what I mean: You have a nagging feeling that you should call your friend Mary. You haven't spoken in months. She lives in a distant city. Acting on this sense, you do phone and discover that Mary has some wonderful news to share with you. How did you know to call? Or take the surprisingly common experience of waking up in the middle of the night and knowing that a loved one is in trouble or that someone close to you has died. This inner connection to a distant other is more than unconscious processing of forgotten memories or subtle clues. Something else is happening. I am told that my brother-in-law, when he was young, knew who was calling when the phone rang. How did he know?

There is a lot of evidence that premonitions of this sort do happen. Although anecdotes are not evidence, the sheer abundance of such incidents gives one pause. And, in fact, there is now scientific evidence that two photons (light particles) can becomes "entangled" so that "when a property of light—such as spin, position, or momentum—was measured in one of the particles, the 'twin' particle instantly showed the opposite property" even thought they were separated by as much as thirty miles (the experimental distance in this case).[3] While such connections take place on a sub-atomic level and do not prove that human beings are connected on some sort of unconscious level, they do indicate that information can be transferred without a hard-wired link. What is going on here?

An even more intriguing question has to do with precognitive dreams: dreaming in detail about events before they have happened. I was talking about the phenomenon of precognitive dreams in a class at Gordon-Conwell Theological Seminary some years ago, using precognitive dreams as a way to get into a discussion of the unconscious. A student excitedly raised his hand. "That happened to me. It was the weirdest thing."

The student, David, went on to tell the class about a dream he had while he was serving as a U.S. Army officer stationed in Ft. Benning, Georgia.[4] It seems that the night before a major training exercise with the Army Rangers he dreamed in great detail about that exercise. He said, "In my dream I vividly remember calling in a medivac mission. I remember very specifically what happened—my best friend was seriously injured on a patrol just as dawn broke. He was carried out of the jungle on a poncho by six other soldiers who were running towards a clearing approximately a quarter mile away. Just as they broke the clearing the helicopter was coming in. Without even touching down, he was loaded onto the helicopter . . . [which] flew a straight line to Martin Army Hospital . . . where a trauma unit was waiting."

David said that the following morning when the operation was underway he got a high-priority radio message that a soldier was suffering from a serious chest injury, possibly a heart attack. They were requesting an urgent medivac. As they called in the soldier's social security number he recognized it as that of his best friend and before they even finished he had radioed in all the vital information to Martin Army Hospital. The patrol gave their coordinates for where the helicopter could land and said they were less than a quarter mile away. It was the only field within four miles. "The chopper made the field just as the patrol broke out of the jungle. They were able to load him, strap him down, and take off within ten seconds. The chopper never touched the ground." His friend was in the hospital less than four minutes later. David goes on: "The sequence of events mirrored nearly identically the dream I had a day and a half earlier. The same person was involved, the same type of situation occurred, and the scenario of events was remarkably similar. I can only believe that because I had gone through these events in detail in my dream the night previously that I was able to save significant time in coordinating this emergency medical mission."

Over the years I have had a number of other students tell similar stories about precognitive dreams. And you can find such dreams mentioned in the literature,[5] all of which raises the question of how precognitive dreams (or premonitions) are possible.

Carl Jung would say that our unconscious, on its deepest levels, links us to realities outside ourselves (including God). So to Jung it is not surprising that we wake up knowing someone close to us is in trouble or that we dream about events yet to happen. If our unconscious is actually linked to realities outside ourselves, this is a possible explanation for precognitive dreams. God is outside the parameters of time and space. In God past, present and future merge in ways we cannot imagine, so a dream of the near future could be possible.

My main interest is not in proposing explanations (which may or may not be true) for such phenomena. What interests me is the reality of hints and intuitions and how these are akin to the phenomenon of the still small voice that we are discussing. The unconscious seems to be the source of a lot of our intuitions that at times are uncanny in their accuracy. But is this from God or just another example of the stunning design of the human mind by God? Or is it both? Does it matter?

The Creative Process

A related phenomenon has to do with the creative process. Writers, for example, speak about "listening to the muse" or finding a kind of inner stillness that allows them to access their ideas and the words to express them. The best writing seems to come from within, and is as much a product of listening as it is of thinking.

For example, when I was working on the Mastering the Basics Bible study series in the 1980s, I found that after I did all my research on a particular passage, the writing often seemed to come together on its own, when I let it. Sure, I had to read widely about any given passage, consult the various resources that aid in unlocking a 2,000-year-old document (in the case of the New Testament), ponder what it all meant and do all the things that a scholar is supposed to do to grasp the meaning of the text. But as for the writing itself, mostly I needed to listen—trusting that in some way all this research would come together so that I would write clearly and persuasively about the passage in question. At times I felt more like a scribe than an author. A few words would come to mind and I would start writing and see where it took me. More than once I wrote continuously for many minutes, and when I stopped and read over the material I was amazed! Where did that come from?

What I am trying to say in all this is that we are capable of accessing inner thoughts, ideas, images, insights and so forth that come to us from various sources, be it the unconscious; hunches, hints or intuitions; or the voices from our past, our culture, our generation or our longings. We call this ability by various names: the creative process, the artistic imagination, premonitions, an inner "knowing." I think that our experience of the still small voice of God is rooted in this God-given human ability to access such inner reality. But I would argue that the still small voice is a distinctive phenomenon. Its defining characteristic, as Willard noted, is that we have no sense that this "voice" comes from us or is generated by us. Rather, it has the sense that it comes from without, or perhaps better, from beyond. Such a "voice" has a sense of otherness to it, much like a mystical experience. And it is rare, not common. Let me illustrate what I mean.

Experiencing the Still Small Voice

I had a particular experience in which I had the unmistakable sense that it was God speaking to me in this way. It happened on retreat. I had taken a class to a retreat center for the day. It was a silent retreat. The challenge for the students was to be open to God in the midst of the silence. This was my personal challenge as well.

On that particular occasion I was wrestling with an issue in my professional life. A certain individual was bringing great pressure to bear upon me, unfairly I thought. I was stressed. I was unproductive. So not surprisingly this was the issue that became the focus of my prayer that day: what was I to do by way of response?

Late in the afternoon, toward the end of the retreat, I was alone in one of the rustic buildings on the property when I heard within me a soft voice. This was not an audible, exterior voice, but it was clear nonetheless. The voice, as I say, was gentle. It was unobtrusive. It was not insistent but it felt "true." "Stand up for yourself," was all I heard. And so in the weeks that followed I did just that, and the whole issue resolved itself. Eventually I got a letter from the other party, apologizing for the pressure he had put upon me.

God's voice? Who can really know? I do know that this insight came to me in the context of a particular question I had been talking to God about. Furthermore, it proved to be just what I needed to resolve a very troubling issue. And the quality of the voice was what I had experienced on a few previous occasions when it seemed as if God were addressing me. I knew the tone, the gentleness, the lack of insistence, the brevity, the sense of rightness about what was said. This was unlike inner hints, hunches or what happens in the creative process. So if it was not "God," it was certainly "of God"—and that is all that matters to me.

I have had other such experiences. For example, after teaching for many years in the New England area I was invited to join the faculty of Fuller Theological Seminary. Should I accept the invitation? If I went to Fuller it would involve a move all the way across the country, leaving behind friends and family, not to mention the challenge of gearing into a whole new educational system. I prayed a lot about this choice over a number of months. Finally I heard that familiar soft and kind voice I had come to associate with the still small voice of God. What I heard was something like this: "I do not care which choice you make. I will be with you in either instance. Each choice will have its own set of consequences/outcomes that will follow."

On one hand, this did not seem very helpful at the time. It did not answer the "tell me what do" question. On the other hand, upon reflection, this unexpected response (unexpectedness is one of the earmarks of the still small voice) was a far better response than the one I thought I wanted. I came to see that the "tell me what to do" prayers were not always the pathway to wholeness. We need to learn to exercise our God-given ability to choose. As we do so we become more fully human, more mature. It is possible that the "tell me what to do" kind of prayers can become a cop-out for not making our own choices so that later, if things go wrong with a choice, who better to blame than God? "I was just doing what God told me to do." This is not the path to wholeness.

Having mentioned these two experiences, I need to add two things. First, how God's voice sounds to others is something only they can know. The tone, the pitch, the volume is an individual experience. I am simply describing my own experience. I suspect that God addresses each of us in ways that are unique to us.

The second thing I need to say is that I am suspicious of those who claim to hear God's voice on a regular, daily basis. I say this not just because I do not experience the still small voice on a daily basis. I am hesitant with the "God told me" folk because my experience with them is that, over time, they seem to have an excessively clear idea of the mind of God on all too many matters. And this confidence that they know God's mind is sometimes tinged with a hint of superiority (they hear; lesser mortals don't). This becomes especially troubling when their "opinions," which they take to be more than mere opinion (in fact they claim that this is the direct leading of God), turns out to sound a lot like the rhetoric of their own group. When this sense of "God told me" spills over into political discourse, for example, it becomes quite frightening. In addition, I am troubled when what comes out of their mouths seems to have a different tone from what I hear in the Bible.

All of which raises the question of discernment. Is that really God you are hearing or is that just your mother's voice in your head? Or is it the voice of culture or of your generation or of your own needs or desires? To say that God can and does address us via the still small voice requires both humility and discernment. I will talk about discernment in the conclusion. It is such an important issue that it requires a longer conversation.

In one of my classes some years ago I expressed my uneasiness with those who claim to hear God speaking all the time, especially when these "messages" are directed at other people. Well, one day not long after that I got a knock on the door of my office. Standing there was a favorite student of mine, a middle-aged African American pastor. He had taken several of my classes. I found him to be thoughtful and caring. I liked who he was and the spirit he brought with him. On that particular day he arrived with a message from God for me. "Now I know, Dr. Peace, that you don't like someone telling you they have a message from God," he began, "and believe me I hesitated before I came here, but I just have to pass this along."

So I listened. What could I do? And, in fact, I listened carefully because I trusted the maturity of this particular person. Later on, when I pondered what he said, I realized his words had the ring of truth to them. Shortly thereafter I went on a two-day private retreat at a nearby Franciscan Retreat Center. I used the time to wrestle with what the student had said as well as to explore certain passages in Scripture that my very perceptive wife (who often has hints and intimations) had suggested might be useful to ponder. Several days after I returned from the retreat, I learned that my mother had died unexpectedly. And the very issues that I looked at on that retreat prepared me to cope with her death.

Retreats as the Place to Listen

Hearing God requires that we listen to God. Finding the time and place in which to do this listening is proving harder and harder. Most of us live in an over-rich sensory environment, filled to the brim with sights, sounds and experiences. We dash from event to event; always wired so we can keep up with what is happening in the world and with our friends. Too much stimulus.

It is hard to hear God's voice in the midst of such a cacophony. If, as I have come to believe, God's voice is usually quiet and unobtrusive, we are apt to miss it with so much inner chatter. So we have to find the right place and time in which to listen. And I have found that retreat centers are the right place for many of us to listen. I mentioned that I had taken a group of students to a one-day silent retreat. I do this regularly in my classes on Christian spirituality. Since it is "required," my students go on retreat and inevitably I get back reports that are highly positive: "I didn't think I had time to spend a day in silence, but once I got to the retreat center I wondered how I survived so long without this kind of rich silence." I have come to believe that silence is central to the revival of interest in spirituality that we are witnessing in the twenty-first century. We need to develop a taste for silence, a comfort in the midst of silence. We also need the tools to reach out to God in that silence as well as the ability to notice God's voice.

Again, if you are interested in this whole concept of the still small voice, it is one thing to read about it and quite another to experience it. So I would suggest that you find a place where you can experience the silence you need.

Dreams, Visions and other Manifestations

What about dreams and visions as ways God might communicate with us on an inner level? I have talked about precognitive dreams, but they are rare. What about ordinary, garden-variety, every-night dreams?

Certainly the Bible indicates that during both the time of the Old Testament and the New Testament—while this may not have been common—divine communication via dreams and visions was certainly the experience of some, like the parents of Jesus. Mary, the mother of Jesus, has a visit from an angel (which qualifies as a vision) explaining that she would bear a child (not the kind of vision a young unmarried woman would welcome). Mary believed what she was told and pondered the meaning of it all. And later Joseph, Mary's husband, was told in a dream (another kind of communication) to flee to Egypt since the life of the baby Jesus was in peril. Joseph believed what he heard and did what was asked, and so Jesus was not present during the awful "slaughter of the innocents" described in Matthew's Gospel (Matthew 2:13-18). As for the apostle Paul while in Troas, "during the night Paul had a vision: there stood a man of Macedonia pleading with him and saying, 'Come over to Macedonia and help us' " (Acts 16:9). Paul did just that and thus the mission to the Gentiles was born, out of which the Western church emerged. You find stories like this throughout the Bible, and we hear the same report from mystics down through the ages. God can and does speak through dreams and visions.

The fact is that we all dream, every night, whether we remember our dreams or not. God created us so that we dream.

Dreams arise from various levels of our unconscious. I have come to believe that on rare occasion God can and does speak through dreams. Like the still small voice, such dreams have a sense of otherness about them. They are "different" from ordinary dreams, even the so-called big dreams that are filled with power for us, arising, as Jungians would say, from the collective unconscious. Again it is a matter of tone that distinguishes these rare God-given dreams. They are generally self-authenticating.

I have had a few such dreams. I am not good at recalling dreams, and while I have gone through periods in my life when I worked at recording dreams, mostly I forget what I dream. But one particular dream woke me up. It came at the time when my work and ministry was bogged down, or so it seemed. I was working at a film studio, and while the work there was interesting and challenging (and it had its moments of creativity), this certainly did not qualify as "ministry" in the way I had come to understand it. (Sure, all forms of work and vocation can be sites of ministry, but this was not the kind of direct, church-oriented ministry to which I thought I had been called and for which I was trained.) I had almost come to the conclusion that I should stop thinking about direct ministry any longer. And furthermore, I was bogged down in my Ph.D. work, which seemed to drag on forever. Why do a Ph.D. in biblical studies if I was not going to be in full-time ministry?

Then I had this dream. It was not an ordinary dream. In the dream I felt God calling me to carry on and, in particular, to finish my Ph.D. I even had a sense out of the dream as to the direction I should take in my research. I woke up. I felt energized. I knew what I needed to do. Soon after that I got a call from Gordon-Conwell Theological Seminary to begin teaching there. The fact that I had a Ph.D. underway was an important reason why I was asked to teach. I wish I could say that I quickly completed the dissertation (it dragged on for quite a few more years). But I did keep working on it and eventually finished. My Ph.D. then unlocked all sorts of new options for me. I suspect I would not have completed it had it not been for that dream in which I heard God speaking to me.

Dreams are tricky, however. Dream language is nonlinear, image-oriented and free from the constraints of space and time. It is often hard to make sense of a dream, except in those rare instances where the dream is self-interpreting. Again, this is an avenue by which God can and does speak, but what we hear in dreams needs to be interpreted carefully in the larger context of our lives.

Conviction

I also think God speaks to us on an interior level via conviction. At times, for example, there is an inner sense of rightness that comes when we are faced with a demanding course of action. We know what we must do. Where that "knowing" comes from is hard to pin down, but it seems to transcend personal preference or community consensus. I have come to feel that this sort of moral imperative can and does come from God and we need to pay attention to such convictions. C. S. Lewis would argue that moral judgments of this sort cannot be merely a product of nonmoral, nonrational Nature, but must, in fact, have their origins in some sort of higher, absolute moral wisdom, which we call God.[6]

Of course, a lot of people have many strong convictions, and that does not make those convictions right, much less divinely inspired. Heaven help us (literally) if this were the case. In this atmosphere of political polarization it would be very dangerous to claim divine sanction just because we feel something strongly. So again, as with all the ways God can potentially address us, we must ponder deeply before we act, much less claim to be led by God. How we ponder such convictions is the subject of the conclusion.

I have come to call a related phenomenon "divine compulsions": the sense of "ought" that convicts us that we must act in a certain way or undertake a certain task. It is important to distinguish between divine compulsions and neurotic compulsions. We have plenty of the latter. But what I have in mind is illustrated by a story told me by a friend in South Africa when we lived there. My friend was a Methodist minister. He had another friend who was also a Methodist minister, and it is her story that he told me.

Apparently one day she was walking down the street in Johannesburg. She saw a man coming toward her on the same side of street, a stranger. At that moment she had the strongest sense come over her that she should speak to him, in fact, that she should say something quite specific to him. This was way outside her normal behavior, much less her comfort zone. But she had no time to ponder her choice. He was walking toward her. When they came together she stopped and said to him: "Sir, don't do it!" He stopped, looked aghast, burst into tears and fell to his knees. "How did you know?" he asked, "how did you know?" Then his story came out. He was on the way to the house of a woman who had rejected him, to do her grave harm and then to take his own life. But this divinely motivated (?) intervention stopped all that. This illustrates what I mean by a divine compulsion. Such stories of "leadings," as my charismatic friends would call them, are not uncommon.

But the question remains: Is the compulsion from God or is its origin in our fears or desires? That is the challenging question. I know some of these same charismatic friends would say that all such convictions are divine convictions. God is calling you to do something that is outside your own comfort zone, so you better do it. Again, I am not sure. Maybe. Maybe not.

Significance

Some years ago I read an article in *Christianity Today* in which one of the editors, who was also a college professor, gave an account of how in October 2005 God had spoken to him. He began by saying that while for him it was theoretically possible that God spoke to people, this had never been his experience. So it came as a great shock one day when this happened to him.

He had been praying about how to find money to help a friend of their family pay for tuition to his very expensive college. Out of the blue a book title came to him. It was so clever, he knew the book would sell well. Not only that, but the outline for the whole book presented itself to him. He was quite excited, needless to say. Although he had published other books, none had to come him in this fashion. He went home and began writing. "As I wrote," he said, "I had the distinct feeling that this was not me. I had never written like this before. The words poured out. Two weeks later, a 200-page manuscript sat on my desk. I knew it was good."

He contacted a publisher. The book was quickly accepted. A handsome royalty was paid to him—ten times more than he had received for any other book. He started thinking about how he would use the royalty money. They desperately needed a new roof on their house. Then God spoke: "It's not your money. It's his," meaning the young man for whom he had been praying. The long and the short of the story is that his friend was able to go to college because of this money.

The college professor mused: "So what does all this mean?

I'm a theologian and I should know. But I can't spin out a fancy theological formula for God's guidance and provision. What I know is that God spoke to me and used a gift he had already given me to provide for a young man being called into his service. . . . So what has this done for me? Probably more than for the young man bound for ministry. We now have a new roof, for one thing, which came under circumstances that can only be described as oddly providential—but that's another story. More importantly, my faith in a living, personal, loving, and providing God has been renewed and deepened. Now I know, more than intellectually, that God still speaks."[7]

In conclusion, I also offer a quotation because it ties together much of what I have been trying to say in the previous two chapters. It is from Theodor Bovet, a highly regarded Swiss physician and psychiatrist:

> When we think about Christ and call on him, it is not as though we were appealing to a dead or an absent person and deliberating about him: Christ answers, he has an effect on us, he is with us, he is alive. This is demonstrated in the fact that his will confronts us with increasing clarity as an absolute, complete, indeed foreign, will, radically different from our own wills. In those moments when we begin to consider Christ, we usually would like to find in him the confirmation of our own personal will, that is to say his plan should bring ours to the highest degree of perfection. But his will emerges in an entirely different context, with a completely new viewpoint, in contrast to which our will appears to be permeated with trivialities and self-seeking motives. . . .
>
> The abrupt antithesis of Christ's will to ours surprises us; we are vexed by this Otherness.

> Here God lays hold of our innermost self. Christ desires that I should tell the definite facts of illness to a patient [in giving this personal illustration Bovet focuses on his role as a medical doctor]; I resist this because I do not wish to be altogether truthful with this person. Christ would enjoin me not to attend a certain movie, for I would like to attend it chiefly for the purpose of arousing licentious feelings. . . . Christ thrusts me continually in to the presence of a certain person; I wish always to evade him because I do not like him and cannot forgive him. Right at this point I need to be changed.[8]

What I am trying to say is that I believe God can and does speak to us via an inner voice. But I also want to say that we must test that voice carefully. It is all too easy to attribute to God what is not of God. It all too easy to make God a crutch. I do not think that God wants to be a crutch. God wants us to grow up, make choices, and live a healthy, productive and fully human life. Yes, God can and does lead us. Yes, we should seek direction from God. But in my experience, a lot of the time we just need to do the right thing. Or we just have to choose. One choice leads one direction. Another choice leads a different direction. And God is with us on either path. The call is not to over-believe or under-believe when it comes to the question of the still small inner voice. The call is to listen and then to act in faith.

4

The Power of Community

Mother Teresa of Calcutta is widely quoted as saying of dying beggars, "Each one of them is Jesus in disguise."[1] How can this be, we might ask? What does she mean? Can we find truly Jesus in others?

The Benedictine Experiment

Let's look first at the Benedictines and their experiment in seeking God together as a community. There are rich clues here as to what it means to meet God in others (as well as insight into ways to be present to God). We need some history in order to understand how monastic communities developed and how they came to be structured as they are.

The monastic movement began in the third century when pious men and women fled to the deserts to seek God in the midst of the deep silence. At first the desert fathers and mothers lived alone in isolation, but over time they gathered together into small communities that eventually became the first monasteries. These monasteries were a kind of oasis as the Dark Ages descended upon Europe.

But how do you structure life together in a monastery? Monks and nuns tended to be quite independent. So who cooks the food? Who does the dishes? And where does the food come from? A lot of practical questions arise when people begin to live in community. But we know this; newly married couples face the same questions.

And the monasteries of the sixth century were like large families, as Esther de Waal points out. Most of them were small groups of about a dozen people.

> The monastery itself would be a small single-storey building, and scattered around would lie offices, outhouses, farm-sheds. Neither dormitory, refectory or oratory needed to be large or elaborate. The cloister was a thing of the future. The small community who gathered here as a Christian family to live, work and pray together would probably make small claim for themselves, for most were simple men, few were priests or scholars. The pattern of the day was established by the *opus Dei,* the work of God, the purpose of the monastic life. So seven times a day the monks would gather in the oratory [to pray]. . . . The rest of the time was fully occupied with domestic or agricultural work, with study and reading, besides two meals and the hours of sleep. Here were men living together to serve God and save their souls, glad to care for those who sought them out but content to remain essentially ignorant of the world outside their walls.[2]

Over time various rules were produced as guides to the organization of monastic communities, but it was the *Rule of St. Benedict* (529?) that eventually became the guide of choice for monasteries. In fact, for six hundred years (from 700 C.E. to 1300 C.E.) the majority of monasteries followed the *Rule of Benedict.* Even today, the order that Benedict founded (which now includes the Benedictines, Cistercians and Trappists) is alive and thriving.

At the heart of the *Rule of Benedict* are two assumptions: first, that the presence of God is everywhere and second, that Christ is to be met in other people.[3] These are, of course, the central issues in this chapter. So the question is, what does a community look like that is organized to facilitate this dual awareness of God?

The answer is that life in a Benedictine monastery is structured so as to enable *mindfulness* of God and *hospitality* to others. In practical terms this means that each day is organized in such a way that time is given over to cultivating the presence of God via the daily offices and *lectio divina* (mindfulness) and time is also given to work of various sorts (along with other monks or nuns), which includes reaching out to guests (hospitality). Thus the Benedictine motto: "*Ora et labora*" (Pray and work). As Columba Stewart says, "The genius of Benedict was to situate the individual search for God within a communal context that shaped as well as supported the quest. For him community was not simply the place where one seeks God but its vital means."[4]

These two aspects of Benedictine community—mindfulness and hospitality—offer ways to get at what it means to find God in others.

Mindfulness

If God is present within a community, the first task is to notice God, to be present to God, to be "mindful" of God. Within a Benedictine community, two spiritual practices in particular seek to foster this awareness of God's presence: the daily offices of prayer and *lectio divina*.

Benedict prescribed eight daily offices of prayer, consisting mostly of Psalms, beginning with vigils at 2:00 a.m. and moving to lauds at 5:00 a.m. and on through the day (prime, terce, sext, none), ending with vespers at 8:00 p.m. and compline at bedtime. Originally the monks spent about three-and-a-half hours in common prayer each day. Today the actual number of offices and the times they meet vary from community to community, but the idea is the same: everyone meets together to recite or chant the Psalms. The goal, originally, was to recite all 150 Psalms weekly. In this way, by praying the church's original prayer book (the Psalms), the community is shaped in accord with the vision of the Psalms, prayer is offered to God via the Psalms, and God speaks to the community through the Psalms. Today an increasing number of individuals on their own engage in fixed-hour prayer, as it is called.[5]

In addition to the common prayer found in the liturgy of the hours, there is individual prayer called *lectio divina* or "sacred reading." This Bible-based form of prayer is "the hallmark of Benedictine spirituality."[6] Benedict expected the monks to spend about three hours a day in private prayer, engaged in *lectio divina*. Over the years *lectio divina* has assumed various shapes and forms, but at its heart is a slow, meditative reading of Scripture that leads to the pondering of certain words or phrases out of which prayer to God flows, ending in contemplative silence before God.

Unlike my contact with Ignatian spirituality, which was guided by my Jesuit spiritual director, my first encounter with *lectio divina* came from books. William Shannon's *Seeing the Face of God* (Crossroad, 1990) described the whole process for me in a way that I understood, and Norvene Vest's *Bible Reading for Spiritual Growth* (HarperSanFrancisco, 1993) explains the process of group *lectio* that I began to try out in various contexts. Even as I was learning this process of prayer for myself, I began sharing it with others (as professors are wont to do). In particular, I started doing group *lectio* in seminars, classes and at conferences. Looking back on this I am amazed that I presumed to lead others in a form of prayer that I myself had only begun to grasp. But no one in my circles seemed to be doing this at the time (at least that I knew of), and most importantly, the process itself is so powerful that even in my bumbling way the response was overwhelmingly positive. People met God in life-changing ways. Scripture came alive for them. Prayer was renewed. They encountered God. In the next chapter, "The Written Word," I will describe in more detail the process of *lectio divina*.

So the very foundation of a Benedictine community was the daily practice of corporate and individual prayer by which one encountered the presence of God. Noticing God in others is built on the foundation of noticing God in life.

Hospitality

One of the most famous lines in *The Rule of St. Benedict* states: "All guests who present themselves are to be welcomed as Christ, for he himself will say: *I was a stranger and you welcomed me* (Matt 25:35)."[7] The Benedictines have long been known for their hospitality. What interests me is that the basis for this hospitality is found in how they view others: Receive others *as if they were Christ*. Esther de Waal explains: "For if we are really to receive everyone as Christ that means that we must respect each as made in the image of God."[8] The Benedictines do not think that the stranger at the gate, the abbot in the monastery, the hungry beggar or anyone else *is* Christ. But they do think that the image of God dwells somehow in each person. And indeed the Bible says that God created humankind in God's own image, and this implies that in some way we each bear traces of that image in ourselves. Quite apart from anything else, if we believe that each person is made in the image of God, this should impact how we treat others. We would seek to treat others as we would treat Jesus. Such is the way of love.

But I think this axiom ("receive others as if they were Christ") goes deeper than just recognizing that all are made in the image of God. Might this not also be saying that *Christ is in all of us* in some way, recognized or unrecognized?

Certainly St. Paul says that we are "in Christ" and "Christ is in us." He was talking about those early followers of Jesus and what it meant to have the life of Christ indwell them. Jesus himself hints at this sort of reality in the so-called parable of the sheep and goats (to which Benedict refers in his call for hospitality). Jesus talks about the end of time and the final judgment:

> Then the king will say to those at his right hand, "Come, you that are blessed by my Father, inherit the kingdom prepared for you from the foundation of the world; for I was hungry and you gave me food, I was thirsty and you gave me something to drink, I was a stranger and you welcomed me, I was naked and you gave me clothing, I was sick and you took care of me, I was in prison and you visited me." Then the righteous will answer him, "Lord, when was it that we saw you hungry and gave you food, or thirsty and gave you something to drink? And when was it that we saw you a stranger and welcomed you, or naked and gave you clothing? And when was it that we saw you sick or in prison and visited you?" And the king will answer them, "Truly I tell you, just as you did it to one of the least of these who are members of my family, you did it to me." (Matthew 25:34-40)

What interests me about this parable is the idea that in giving to the needy (the hungry, the thirsty, the homeless, the poor, the sick and the imprisoned) we are giving to Christ—whether we know it or not. The other thing that strikes me is that in each instance this involves an act of service to persons in need, service that deals with the most basic issues: the need for food and drink, the need for a place to stay, the need for clothing, the need for nursing when ill, the need for comfort when in prison. The church has long understood this to be the duty of love.

But still the question is, what does it mean to meet Christ in the other?

According to David Robinson, Benedict is talking about the incarnational presence of Christ in our midst. By faith, Benedict takes Jesus' word literally that "just as you did it to one of the least of these who are members of my family, you did it to me." Benedict is not play-acting, pretending that the other is Christ, knowing full well he or she is not. Rather, Benedict really believes that somehow Christ is in each of us, so much so that he instructs his monks that in the presence of a guest they are to bow their heads or lie prostrate before the guest "as a way of adoring Christ present in the guest." Robinson goes on to say, "Benedict affirms the Biblical vision of Emmanuel, God with us, Christ in our midst, the Emmaus road Stranger walking alongside us with our eyes often veiled to recognize his presence. Benedict affirms the mystery of Christ's presence in our midst, fully believing Christ loves to show up, over and over, especially among 'the least of these,' among guests, the poor, the sick, and pilgrims." This accords with the view of Augustine and others that "Christ is present and active in the human soul long before we are aware or willing to accept this gift."[9]

As Columba Stewart points out: "Benedict's most fundamental insight in the *Rule* is that we seek God through ordinary means. God is already here, in and among us, if only we can learn to see Christ and hear his voice in those with whom we live."[10]

Regardless of how we understand (or fail to understand) what it means for us to meet Christ in the other, the practical outcome is quite clear: Love other people. Especially love the stranger, the pilgrim and the needy among you. In doing so you will be loving Christ. This is in accord with the Great Commandment given by Jesus: love God wholeheartedly and love others (as we love ourselves). There is a deep and powerful connection between loving others and loving God/Christ. No separation. The two directions of love comingle. Mother Teresa said, "God still loves the world through you and through me today."[11] We are instruments of God's love. People know God's love via us. We know God's love through others. This is a core truth.

Andrew Greeley says that we live in a grace-filled world whereby all manner of objects—fire, water, sun, mountain, moon—have the potential to stir up grace (more about this in chapter six). But primarily it is other people through whom we encounter grace and experience hope.[12] As we hear stories of love, faith, hope, goodness and kindness in the lives of others—both those who are with us now and those who live on in our shared tradition—so we are provoked to enter into these same realities, to display these traits, to open ourselves to these experiences. Thus we begin to act kindly toward others (for example), and so grow more kind in spirit, even as we touch the loving kindness of the Other.

All this is easier said than done. Even in monastic communities (which I do not want to idealize) there are relational problems of all sorts. For this reason Benedict ends the *Rule* with a very realistic discussion of the challenges of living in community, discussing such things as grumbling, gossiping and fighting. He should know how difficult life could be in a monastery. When as a young monk he was drafted (somewhat unwillingly) to be the abbot of a small monastery, he was (apparently) so strict that after a while the monks actually tried to poison him to get rid of him. Seeing Christ in others will always be a challenge![13]

The New Testament is concerned with the issue of how to build true community. When I first started reading the Bible I was struck by how much space was taken up in the Epistles with this question of getting along with one another. I suppose I had an idealized view of the early church. After all, they were the ones who had got it right and whom we needed to emulate. These were the very churches that had been founded by those who knew Jesus. Of course, they would be perfect!

In fact, a more mature reading of the text makes it clear that the early church was every bit as messy as the church today. In Corinth, for example, a young man had to be warned against sleeping with his mother-in-law, and other believers in that church were admonished about taking each other to court. In some New Testament churches the Lord's Supper had turned into a raucous meal in which the rich ate and drank abundantly (they even got drunk), while the poorer members of the church had little or nothing to eat. No wonder we get all the instructions in the Epistles about how to live together successfully!

But despite the struggles, community is the laboratory in which we learn to love and be loved. And hospitality lies at the heart of community even as mindfulness forms the heart of being present to God in that community.

Spiritual Fruit

How do we recognize Christ in others? This is the challenge. Is this an act of faith: we just believe that Christ is present in the other? Is this a matter of recognition: in them via their acts and attitudes we see traces of Jesus? Is this an encounter with their pilgrimage: we see Christ in their unfolding stories? Is this all of the above?

I have found that there are two specific ways in which we encounter Christ in others: by means of spiritual fruit and through the experience of spiritual gifts.

By spiritual fruit I mean those traits mentioned by St. Paul in Galatians 5:22-23, namely, love, joy, peace, patience, kindness, goodness, faithfulness, gentleness and self-control. I think this list is meant to be representative, not complete. Other "fruit" is mentioned in the New Testament such as humility and hope. In any case, what Paul describes here are those inner attitudes (graces, virtues) that express themselves in our relationships with others. This list describes who we are meant to become, by God's grace.

We also need to notice that such fruit is the work of the Holy Spirit. This is not natural fruit. Such fruit reflects or manifests the work of the Holy Spirit. As such, when we manifest these graces in ourselves or when we touch these graces in others, we are to some degree in touch with the energy of the Holy Spirit. Such traits, of course, produce positive relationships and are the foundation of vital community life.

Paul sets this good fruit in the context of bad fruit (though he does not use the phrase "bad fruit"). In the prior passage (Galatians 5:16-21) he lists "the deeds of the lower side of human nature,"[14] namely, "fornication, impurity, licentiousness, idolatry, sorcery, enmities, strife, jealousy, anger, quarrels, dissensions, factions, envy, drunkenness, carousing, and things like these." The bad fruit, as I am calling it, drags us down, disrupts community and makes us less than we were meant to be. As such, it is to be shunned. "Do not gratify the works of the flesh." We all know the moral conflict between positive and negative desires. Leaving behind the bad fruit and grasping the good fruit is one way of understanding the process of Christian transformation: becoming God calls us to be, becoming who we long to be.

' so when we encounter any of this good fruit in others,

to some degree we encounter the work of the Spirit, the presence of Christ and the reality of God. As Jesus says in Matthew 7:15-20, "you will know them by their fruits." Likewise, when we display such fruit to others, so too we are expressing the reality of transcendence. Where does such love, joy or peace in us come from? On one level this is the best of who we are; but on another level, these traits have their origin in God. Have we not all had, for example, an irrational sense of hope in the midst of circumstances that should not inspire hope and known that such hope is a gift to us?

I believe we see Christ in others when we encounter the fruit of the Spirit.

So it would be helpful, I think, to examine more closely each of these traits as a way of grasping what we look for in others and seek to cultivate in ourselves.

- *Love.* St. John makes the affirmation in his first epistle that "God is love" (1 John 4:7-8). It is not that God brings love (though God does), not that God promotes love (God does), not that God desires for us to be in loving relationships (though God does). It is that God, in God's essence, is Love. Thus, where love prevails, in some way God is present. Greek has four words translated by the single English word "love." In the Galatians text the word used is *agape,* which refers to a kind of active reaching out to others simply because they are in need, without regard to reward or response. It is this kind of love that God inspires in us and in others.

- *Joy* is not the same as happiness. Rather, it refers to a kind of deep inner attitude of delight. This sort of joy is not disturbed by hardship. It is connected with hope that knows there is an inheritance waiting for us in God's future. For example, in Paul's letter to the Philippians the word "joy" is used twenty-three times, despite the fact that Paul is in a horrendous situation. He is under house-arrest, chained twenty-four hours a day to one of the imperial guards. Paul, the great activist with a burning passion to spread the gospel message throughout Europe, is forced to stay put day after day as he awaits his sentence from the imperial court. Furthermore he may not prevail in his case. He may be sentenced to death. If all this were not bad enough, some of Paul's Christian critics are taking advantage of his incarceration to demean Paul and challenge his ministry. All this must have been very hard on Paul, and yet what he writes about is joy. His life in Christ has transcended his situation.

- *Peace* is not contentment as much as it is a deep inner centeredness. The prime meaning of this word is not negative—"an absence of conflict—but positive: "the presence of that which brings wholeness and well-being." The presence that brings such peace is God.
- *Patience* is the ability to hang in there with people who aggravate or persecute you. It is the ability to bear up under stress. This is not a natural trait!
- *Kindness* is an attitude toward people, a way of relating to others with care and thoughtfulness for the other's needs and feelings.
- *Goodness* is closely related to kindness. It is, perhaps, a more active way to relate to others in word and deed.
- *Faithfulness* is the character trait of reliability; the faithful person is someone you can depend upon.
- *Gentleness* is another character trait: it is a kind of meekness, though not in the spineless way that word is often understood. It is the ability to defuse tension or conflict.

- *Self-control* is the ability to master the desire and compulsion of the self for gratification.

Each of the first three virtues (love, joy, peace and, by implication, hope) finds its root in God. To display these qualities is to be touched by (in touch with) God. So when we encounter these virtues in other people we encounter God's Spirit at work. The second three virtues (patience, kindness, goodness) are expressed in relationship to other people. They are signs of love in action. Again, as such, they give evidence of the work of the Spirit. The third set of virtues (faithfulness, gentleness and self-control) is more personal in nature. They describe one's inner character as wrought by the work of the Spirit.

Spiritual Gifts

Spiritual fruit involves character traits. Spiritual gifts are skills or abilities given by the Holy Spirit to be used for the sake of others. There are several lists in the New Testament naming various spiritual gifts.[15] Each list is representative, not complete. The gifts named in the New Testament include such things as hospitality, voluntary poverty, prophecy, teaching, being a pastor, evangelism, exhortation, celibacy, giving, leadership, mercy, service, administration, discernment, faith, healing, speaking in tongues, knowledge, wisdom and miracles. This is not the place to explore the nature and use of each of these gifts. It is just to say that we are each called to reach out to others by means of those gifts and skills we have in order to build up each other, to help each other, to serve each other. Again, this is the way of love.

And how is it that we meet God via the exercise of such gifts? Well, take the gift of healing, for example. It is a powerful experience to have a person with the gift of healing pray for you and then discover that, contrary to normal medical expectations, you recover from your illness. I suspect that it is an equally powerful experience to be the one who prays for the healing of another. In both instances, the giving and the receiving, all one can say is, "This is not me. This is from God."

Or take a less dramatic example. Teaching is listed as a gift from God, and I think we all know the power of a gifted teacher—how we are enriched, moved to a new place in our understanding, shown new options for life. This is, of course, what God wants for each of us—to grow into all we are meant to be—and teachers help us do this. When we are on the receiving end of such a gift we see Christ in another.

When we are on the giving end of this gift we also experience the power of God. For example, I can remember certain lectures, addresses and sermons when it felt almost as if what I spoke came from somewhere else. Sure, I had prepared—both in terms of reading and reflection over the years but also in terms of having crafted this particular lecture—but something else was happening. Ideas came together in new ways. New insights emerged that went beyond what I had prepared. New words presented themselves (just the right words); new illustrations came to the surface. I learned even as I spoke. And there was an energy in the room that was palpable. When it was all over I had to ask, where did that come from? I was grateful to have been there, to have been used in that way, to be in touch with the one guiding me.

Some would say that spiritual gifts are given at conversion to be used in the context of the church. Furthermore, they say that these gifts are new and unexpected. These are not the same as natural talents. I do not find this sharp distinction in the New Testament. I think we all have God-given abilities, some by virtue of our genes, our upbringing and our training. But clearly other gifts seem to have a supernatural source. The gift of healing falls into the latter category. No matter the origin of the gifts, t[illegible] im-portant thing is that they be used for the sake of others.

Spiritual gifts are an avenue through which we can sense the presence of God.

Community

The monastery is a particular form of community that can offer insight into how we meet God in others. The Benedictines feel that community is a vital means by which to seek and know God. They structure their daily lives accordingly. But most of us do not live in such intentional communities that make the search for God central to our schedules. We do, however, live in other communities: families, churches, neighborhoods, work places and so on. The challenge is to translate the monastic insights into daily life.[16] What can we learn from the Benedictines that will enrich our quite different communities and make them places where God is found?

For one thing, the principle of mindfulness can function in all circumstances. Simply to ask the question, Where is God in the here and now? enables us to respond to that Presence. To be present to God in all circumstances makes us into a different sort of people. And then when we add the second element of seeing Christ in others, this shapes how we treat others. These two attitudes—seeing God in all things and seeing Christ in others—transfer to all circumstances.

I think it is easy enough to see how powerful it would be if we were to treat those within our communities *as if Christ was present in them*. Our relationships would be transformed. Likewise, to be in touch with the stories of one another's spiritual journeys provides another way of encountering God's presence in the lives of others. Hospitality to others opens avenues for such encounters. Likewise, service to others (the "cup of cold water") is a way to do to others as to Christ.

Intentionality is crucial to the transfer of monastic attitudes into other communities. We need to create spaces within which we can share our stories, discuss our stories and grow together in our spiritual journeys. For example, for some years my wife and I had a small group Bible study that met in our home on a weekly basis. Exploration of various biblical texts gave us the opportunity to discuss our own life journeys as they unfolded.

I think that an understanding of spiritual gifts and fruit casts insight on the nature of the communities we seek to create as individuals striving to follow Christ. Our community life together is the space within which we express and experience the grace of love, joy and peace that comes from God; the attitudes of patience, kindness and goodness toward each other; and the traits of faithfulness, gentleness and self-control that bring wholeness. All these are gifts of the Holy Spirit. Furthermore, in community we find the place in which we can express and experience the spiritual gifts that have been given to all who follow Christ. Many of these gifts build up the body—teaching, discernment, leadership, exhortation and cheerfulness, for example. Other gifts reach out beyond the community—service, hospitality, compassion and healing. It is the gifts and fruit of the Holy Spirit that create the kind of community within which the life of God is evident.[17]

The end result of living in communities that are intended to increase the likelihood that we will notice God is an increased likelihood that we will bear spiritual fruit and utilize spiritual gifts. It will always be a challenge to grow in love of one another; we can start by learning how to see Christ in others.

5

The Written Word

I, for one, would like a world in which the mystical was normal, in which God was made known constantly for all to see. Wouldn't it be great to have a nightly broadcast from God, perhaps etched into the sky at sunset? Then we would know what was really going on and what was expected of us. No fumbling around, wondering, searching, pondering. God would be in charge, we would know it, and all we'd have to do was follow what God said.

But, alas, that is not the way God operates on our planet. Were this the norm, I suspect we would have little need for faith. We would just "know." But without the kind of world in which God speaks directly and continuously, we are forced to learn to listen to the hints and whispers of God coming to us in a variety of ways. We walk by faith, not by sight, St. Paul tells us.

The good news is that we do have an ample record of God's interaction with our planet and the people on it, to which we can turn for insight into God. Christians call this record the Bible, the written Word of God. As such the Bible serves as our guide in our search to know God. In the Bible we find the revelation of who God is, how we can meet and know God, what reality is all about, and how best to live in order to become what we were meant to be (and long to be). "The entire Bible is a record of God's speaking in human history."[1] You want to know God? Begin with the Bible.

So how does the Bible help us notice God? How does the Bible serve as an avenue to God? How do we access the written Word in ways that lead to God? These are the questions this chapter addresses.

The Power of Scripture

I found it hard to write this particular chapter. The difficulty has been to find a way to express the powerful impact Scripture has on people who come to it with open minds and open hearts. The Bible can and does reveal God to us in a way no other text does. Christians talk about the Bible being inspired, something I believe deeply, not just as an article of faith but out of my own experience.

I remember my years of work on the Gospel of Mark (when I was doing my Ph.D.). At first glance Mark presents itself as a rather simple, straightforward exposition of the life of Christ—easy to read, easy to understand. But after a deeper reading, the complexity of its argument, couched in the simplicity and accessibility of its words, is striking. The exposition works seamlessly and simultaneously on multiple levels, like a great symphony with a core theme that is amplified by multiple subthemes, which weave in and out to give it color, shape and substance. I can remember sitting in amazement at what Mark, the author, had written, given the strictures within which he had to write. He could only repeat the stories about Jesus that had circulated in the Christian community for years. He could not add editorial comment except for the odd sentence here and there. His only tool was juxtaposition—arranging the stories side-by-side so that one interpreted another and together they made an argument that was far richer than the sum of the individual stories. Mark was clearly inspired. And that was the point. If I had not already believed in the inspiration of the Bible, my experience of seeing the elegant structure of Mark's Gospel would have led me to that conclusion.[2]

How does one capture the freshness of Scripture, the sense of wonder that it can convey, the impact of the stories as we bring our lives to it, the sense that we are touching true truths here? It seems almost mundane to write about the Bible as a way by which God is revealed to us. In fact, it is the primary avenue by which we encounter God. It shapes our understanding of all other God-encounters. In the end, all I can do is invite you to enter the world of Scripture on your own and see what happens.

The Voice of Jesus

Apart from anything else, it is in the Bible that we meet Jesus. The first four books of the New Testament (the Gospels) tell the story of Jesus. Sure, the Epistles and various non-biblical sources make references to Jesus, but these are for the most part brief or fragmentary. We get the real story in the Gospels. Without the Gospel accounts we would not know Jesus nor would we hear the voice of Jesus.

In chapter two I talked about encountering Jesus by means of our inner imagination. But who is this Jesus we encounter? Is it the Jesus of history or is it a mix of Gandalf, Santa Claus and Superman? It is very important to know all we can know about Jesus before we engage in such a thing as Ignatian contemplation. And in order to encounter the Jesus of history, we have no choice but to turn to the Bible. In the Gospels (Matthew, Mark, Luke and John) we read the words of Jesus; we listen to the teaching of Jesus; we watch Jesus interact with all manner of people from his disciples to his family to his enemies; we see Jesus make choices, choose friends, navigate through the hostile world of first-century Israel filled with its power structures and intrigue. It is in the Gospels that the person of Jesus comes alive for us as four different narrators tell his story, each with a particular slant.

The Gospels are easy to read and quite accessible for the most part. The first Gospel to be written, the one by Mark that I have already mentioned, is the length of a feature article in a magazine like *The Atlantic*. It can be read at one sitting. What emerges from such a reading is the fascinating, enigmatic, frustrating, kind and loving, fierce and challenging person we call Jesus. He is quite different from the sanitized version of Jesus found in contemporary culture. And here is the thing: when we encounter Jesus we are encountering what God looks like in human form.

Barbara Bradley Hagerty, the NPR reporter who wrote *Fingerprints of God,* talks about her experience of reading the Gospels following a mystical experience she had:

> The Gospels—which tell of the kindness and boldness and humanness of Jesus—reached up and grabbed me, demanded that I pay attention. The words of Matthew the tax collector, Mark the itinerant, Luke the doctor, and John the fisherman hijacked my senses. I *heard* the voice of Jesus saying to the prostitute, "Neither do I condemn you, go and sin no more"—I heard it as if he had uttered those words to me. I *tasted* the salty air of the Galilean Sea and *smelled* the fear of the fishermen caught in a vicious squall. When Jesus touched the desperate leper, I recoiled from the brackish wounds. This two-thousand-year-old

> story sprung, like those pop-up birthday cards, from two dimensions to three—from myth to concrete reality.
>
> What unnerved me was that this feeling seemed to come from outside me, not within: it was as if someone had tied a rope around my waist and pulled me slowly and with infinite determination, toward a door that was ajar.[3]

Hagerty then goes on to tell how she opened herself to this God to whom she was being drawn: "I prayed—and in that split second of surrender, I felt my heart stir and grow warm, as if it were changing. It was a physical thing, exquisite, undeniable."[4]

So Jesus is the place to begin if we are to form a right conception of God and a real connection to God.

The Nature of God

But the Bible is much more than just the four Gospels. In the rest of this big, sprawling and often confusing book that contains the work of scores of different people written over the span of hundreds of years, we read about God's ongoing interaction with our planet. On one level, the Bible is the story of humanity's unfolding consciousness of who God truly is. In the beginning, as described in Genesis, there is direct, one-on-one interaction with God, but the innocence of that primal relationship is soon lost. Then the story becomes a matter of helping humanity grow out of a tribal understanding of God ("he is our God, not your God, and this God likes us best") into a full understanding that "God is light" and "God is love," as one of the last books of the Bible declares (1 John).

It is hard—impossible really—to summarize what we find in the Bible concerning this unfolding interaction between God and humanity over the span of all those years, much less to hone in on the question of the Bible as an avenue for encountering God. So let me just identify, in broad strokes, some of what we find in the Bible.

The story of God. God has been involved with this planet right from the beginning, interacting with nations and families and individuals. As we read these stories we begin to get a sense of who God is, how God meets people, and thus where to look for God. Furthermore, we learn the meaning of our own lives as we watch how people in the Bible ponder their God-encounters.

Let me give you an example of what we learn when we listen carefully to the experience of others. Peter, the apostle, is a person who crops up often in the New Testament. He is one of the first ones chosen to be a disciple of Jesus. He becomes the de facto leader of the twelve apostles. He is brash and bold, one minute declaring (at the Last Supper) that he is willing to go with Jesus to prison and even to death (Luke 22:33) and then a few hours later, when confronted by a serving girl in the courtyard of the high priest's house, denying that he even knows Jesus (Luke 22:54-62)—as Jesus predicted he would. But all that begins to change. After the resurrected Lord meets with Peter, he gains a new boldness. He preaches openly in the temple area declaring that Jesus has been raised from the dead, annoying the very same leaders who got Jesus killed in the first place and in the process getting himself arrested (Acts 4:1-3). Peter becomes a leader of the early church. He has a vision from which he learns that God loves the Gentiles whom he hated. So he baptizes a devout Gentile named Cornelius, a Roman centurion of the Italian Cohort and because of this Peter is called to account by scandalized Jewish believers (Acts 10–11). Peter goes on to write several letters that are incorporated into the New Testament, and he is probably the voice behind the Gospel of Mark, the first written account of the life of Jesus.

How does Peter relate to us? For one thing, in Peter we see ourselves, we see our inconsistencies, our brashness, our prejudices, our capabilities. We see how Peter was loved in the midst of his humanness and how the teaching of Jesus and the power of the Holy Spirit changed him over time. In this way the Bible acts as a kind of mirror for us. We learn about ourselves from the story of Peter as we see ourselves in him. We learn about the process of change as we see Peter transformed and so open ourselves to the same transforming process.

This is just one story of hundreds of stories in the Bible from which we learn about how God interacts with human beings and brings about change in their lives, and by extension, change in our lives. The Bible is a guidebook that leads us to God.

The wisdom of God. Here is where we learn how we are meant to live. We also begin to see events from a new perspective. We gain insight into what is happening around us and how to respond. The Bible is a remarkable source of wisdom and has been so down through the ages. Certain sections of the Bible are given over to conveying wise insights (e.g., Proverbs). Other sections teach us directly as we listen in on how God guides the people of Israel or how Jesus teaches the people in the first century. Jesus' Sermon on the Mount (Matthew 5–7), which begins with the amazing Beatitudes, provides ethical guidelines that help us navigate the complex waters of relationships. In the New Testament letters, Paul, the apostle, teaches us how to build and maintain a warm, viable community of Jesus-followers (e.g., Ephesians 4–6 and Romans 12–13).

Why is this wisdom literature so valuable to us? Well, if we understand God to be our creator and the Bible to be the record of God's revelation to us, it makes sense to follow what God has inspired biblical writers to say. The Bible functions as a kind of user's manual for human beings, inspired by the one who created us, telling us how we are meant to function in order to become whole people who live life to the full. It is remarkable how often, when we come to the Bible with open hearts, that we encounter wisdom that renews us. The Bible is an avenue to the wisdom of God.

For example, here is one story:

> I understood why people call the Bible, "the living Word." This is no idle metaphor. Words, when they are infused with the Spirit, can speak across thousands of years, across continents, against all odds. The words of Paul can speak to a 13-year-old girl with inevitable body image issues and say, "Do you not know that your body is a temple?" I read this at exactly the moment I needed to hear it. These words reoriented me. They helped me shed messages of self-depreciation, accumulated over time from a world which exalted impossible beauty and constructed perfection.[5]

The praise of God. Here is where we find the hymns and prayers that have been used for centuries in reaching out to God in worship and thanksgiving. Here is where we learn to respond to God. As we join in the centuries-old prayers, hymns and rituals, so we stay connected to God. We join in the long tradition of response to God. I will say more about all this in chapter seven when I discuss the idea of noticing God in the church.

The Bible is the guidebook that opens up to us the work and character of God. It helps us see God. It enables us to distinguish between God and other realities. It alerts us to the ways of God. We learn to distinguish God's voice from other voices, God's ways from other ways, God's demands (the demands of love) from competing demands. The Bible helps us to know what to look for as we seek God and how then to respond to the God we meet.

God-Encounters in the Bible

The God-encounters recorded in the Bible provide particularly valuable information for us in that they alert us to how God presented himself to other people in history. Without such a record we would wonder about our own mystical encounters. Is it God we met? The mystical encounters in the Bible help us discern the characteristics of such encounters.

So let's look at some of these mystical encounters described in the Bible. Here is just a sampling of God's appearances as recorded in the Old Testament.

God appears to Abraham, the father of three great religious traditions (Genesis 15). In this particular encounter, Abraham first has a vision in which God speaks to him, reaffirming that he will give Abraham a son and heir whose descendants will be as numerous as the stars. Next, God causes a deep sleep to fall upon Abraham, during which God appears and speaks to him, making a covenant with him.

God appears to Moses, the one who led the people of Israel out of Egypt and forward to the Promised Land (Exodus 3). God appears in a burning bush (flames of fire) and speaks to Moses, revealing his true name (nature) to Moses.

God appears to the people of Israel as they were fleeing Egypt (Exodus 13). God appears as a pillar of cloud during the day and a pillar of fire at night, protecting them from the advancing Egyptian army.

God appears again to Moses, this time on Mount Sinai (in what became the paradigmatic appearance narrative) out of which came the Ten Commandments (Exodus 19). The text is worth quoting:

> Now Mount Sinai was wrapped in smoke, because the LORD had descended upon it in fire; the smoke went up like the

> smoke of a kiln, while the whole mountain shook violently. As the blast of the trumpet grew louder and louder, Moses would speak and God would answer him in thunder. When the LORD descended upon Mount Sinai, to the top of the mountain, the Lord summoned Moses to the top of the mountain, and Moses went up. (Exodus 19:18-20)

The appearances continue in the New Testament. God appears as a voice at the baptism (Mark 1:9-11) and transfiguration of Jesus (Matthew 17:1-8). The Holy Spirit comes to the early Christian community with tongues of fire and in the sound of violent wind at the feast of Pentecost (Acts 2). Then there is the amazing conversion of Paul (Acts 9; 22; 26) that we looked at in chapter one.

All these appearances share some common characteristics. For one thing, they all come at the initiative of God. You cannot order-up, as it were, a mystical experience. Second, the appearances are fleeting, unlike the revelation of God that is written into nature. Third, God's self-disclosure brings new insight or new empowerment that changes the nature of things. Fourth, when God comes, nature is rocked with wind, fire, thunder or earthquake. Fifth, even as God reveals himself, so too God conceals himself (in cloud, in storm). Who could stand before the raw presence of God? A mere flash is overwhelming. Sixth, the most common human response to such epiphanies is fear and awe. Finally, God appears for the purpose of self-disclosure. God speaks.[6]

As a result of all these appearance the people of the Bible come to know that God is a "living God." On Sinai the people of Israel "heard the voice of the living God" speaking out of the fire with power and truth (Deuteronomy 5:26). When they cross over into the Promised Land it is declared that "among you is the living God" (Joshua 3:10). The living God is celebrated and sought in the Psalms: "my heart and my flesh sing for joy to the living God" (Psalms 84:2) and "My soul thirsts for God, for the living God" (Psalms 42:2). Christians too come to understand that they are "children of the living God" (Romans 9:26), who follow Jesus Christ, "the Son of the living God" (Matthew 16:16).[7]

The declaration that God is a living God drives our own search for God. God is not a dead abstraction of the philosophers nor a tribal deity defined by the few; nor is God the mere product of our wishful thinking. God is alive: energetic, knowable, active in this world, full of power and mysterious, especially mysterious. It is Mystery we seek and Mystery we encounter, before which we stand in gratitude, awe and wonder, as have women and men down through the ages, so the Bible tells us.

Encountering God in the Bible

It is one thing to *read about God* in the Bible. That, in itself, is powerful. But we can also *meet God* in the Bible. What I mean here is that the Bible, at times, seems to come alive on us and we encounter God in its pages in a special way. Let me tell you about one such experience I had.

It was the end of my freshman year at college. One Sunday I attended an evening service at a local church. It was Missionary Sunday. I had always enjoyed hearing from missionaries. As far as I was concerned they were the contemporary heroes and heroines of faith. That evening several missionaries spoke. They told us about their work in foreign countries. They challenged us to become missionaries ourselves. The pastor gave an invitation at the conclusion of the service for those who felt called to become missionaries to come forward to declare their intent. I did not respond to this invitation. I had never felt myself called to be a missionary. But I had been energized by the service.

When I returned to my dorm room that evening, a strange thing happened. I felt this strong compulsion to pick up my Bible and read it—then and there. It was like I had no choice. So I went to my desk, opened my Bible at random (something I never did—my Bible study was systematic) and started reading. I say "reading" but it was more akin to "listening." The words I saw on the page had the quality of spoken words, words that were addressed to me.

The passage to which I had turned was Matthew 28:16-20, the so-called Great Commission, although at the time I did not know it as such. The passage describes how after the death of Jesus the eleven disciples return to Galilee where the resurrected Jesus had told them to go. Jesus meets them there and the disciples worship him (which was the only possible response given that he had died and was now risen from the dead). But at the end of the verse describing this, there is an odd phrase, "but some doubted." I was struck by that phrase. How could they doubt (remember, these are the very disciples of Jesus) when the resurrected Jesus was standing right before their eyes? (Later I reflected that this was the choice I was being given in this experience: to worship or to doubt.)

The next words are the ones that really got me. Jesus says to them—but I also heard him saying this to me—"Go therefore and make disciples of all nations, baptizing them in the name of the Father and of the Son and of the Holy Spirit, and teaching them to obey everything that I have commanded you" (Matthew 28:18-20). These words were electric, and they were directed to me. I understood Jesus to be calling me to be a missionary.[8]

I never had an experience quite like this again. There have been times, many times in fact, when the Bible was rich with meaning, but the luminescence of that moment was unique. Out of it came my call to ministry.

Encountering God in the Bible: Focused Study and Active Reflection

I don't think we can go to the Bible and expect it to come alive for us in this way, except on rare moments given by God. But I do think that the Bible can be for us, literally, the Word of God, if we let it. The challenge is to open ourselves to the text.

I want to suggest a two-part process by which to approach the Bible. Part one involves *focused study;* part two involves *active reflection.*

First, the study part. Apart from anything else we need to understand the Bible. After all, the New Testament was written two thousand years ago. The Hebrew Scriptures are even older. To read an ancient text as if it were a contemporary text is to court misunderstanding. Fortunately a lot of tools are available to us that enable us to grasp what the Bible is saying in its original context. Bible dictionaries, atlases, reference works and commentaries abound. The challenge is to use these tools wisely.

The temptation is to grab a commentary and see what a scholar has to say about the passage we are reading. I want to suggest that we should only go to commentaries after we have read, and reread, and read again the passage in question. We need to read until we grasp what is being said there. Then we need to figure out the meaning of what we have read. One fruit of our reflection should be a series of questions about the text: about its social context, about what certain words mean, about names and places in the passage—information we need in order to understand what is *really* going on in a passage. This is the time to consult commentaries: with questions in hand to which we need answers. As we work at understanding the Bible, using the tools available to us, eventually we "get it." We understand what is being said and why.

Perhaps the best way to study the Bible is with a group of like-minded friends, using material written to guide such a small group conversation.

This is important. Unless you understand what the Bible is actually saying, you may just read into the text something that is not there. Just look at all those odd sects claiming impossible things derived from their idiosyncratic reading of the Bible. This can be very dangerous, in fact, trapping individuals into a kind of cultic view of God that diminishes life. This is not to say we always get it right when we study the Bible, but over time, with the help of others, listening to thoughtful sermons, in a church with good teachers, we can and do grasp the meaning of the Bible.

But this study and understanding is not enough. It provides a good beginning, but we need to go one step further. We need to open ourselves to what the Bible is saying to us as people seeking to know and follow God. Otherwise we are standing on the outside looking in as disinterested scholars gathering information when what we really need to do is let ourselves be transformed by what we read. This is the second part of the process: active reflection.

There is an ancient form of Bible reading (which can be traced back to the Benedictines) that seeks to bring us into just such a transformative relationship with the Bible. Called *lectio divina* ("sacred reading"), this approach assumes that God wants to speak to us from the Bible. Part one in encountering the Bible is study—a left-brain analytic activity. Part two is conscious reflection—a right-brain creative response. We need both parts. Analysis alone can lead to an arid scholasticism that makes little difference to how we live. Reflection alone can lead to an irresponsible subjectivism that makes us do crazy things. We need to listen to the Bible with both mind and heart. We need to listen to what the Bible says and what the Bible is saying to us.

Lectio divina is a four-step process.

Step one is reading or listening. Read aloud a short passage of Scripture. As you do so, listen for the word or phrase that speaks to you from the passage. What is the Holy Spirit drawing your attention to?

Step two is meditating. Repeat aloud the word or phrase to which you are drawn. Make connections between it and your life at this point in time. What is God saying to you by means of this word or phrase?

Step three is praying. Take these thoughts, meditations and ideas and offer them back to God in prayer, giving thanks for God's guidance and resting in God's love for you. What is God asking you to pray?

Step four is contemplating. Move from the activity of prayer to the stillness of contemplation. Simply rest in God's presence. Stay open to God. Listen for God. Listen to God. Remain in peace and silence before God. How is God revealing himself to you?

Lectio divina really is that simple and that challenging. It is easy to learn, easy to practice. Probably the best way to do it is with others. Group *lectio* involves sitting in a circle with four or five other people. A short passage of Scripture is read aloud several times. Each person listens for the word or phrase that strikes him or her. Then they go around the circle and share that word or phrase aloud. The passage is read aloud again and the group spends a few minutes in silent reflection asking, How does this word or phrase connect with my life? After a time, go around the circle a second time and allow each person to share briefly the connections each sees. The passage is read aloud again followed by more silent reflection, this time asking, Am I being called upon to respond in some way in the next few days to what I heard? More sharing follows, along with prayer for one another, ending with a debriefing of the whole experience.[9]

Lectio divina can lead to a powerful encounter with Scripture. Of course, as with any subjective experience, we need to weigh what we hear, adding to it other insights, including discussion with friends. This is the process of discernment (which I will discuss in the conclusion). Over time clarity comes and we can confidently move in a God-ward direction. The important thing is to listen deeply to Scripture. An unreflective life leaves us at the mercy of cultural winds and currents, not to mention the seductive voices of the advertisers that haunt our culture. We need a wise source outside our culture and ourselves in our search for God.

Significance

So how is the Bible an avenue to the presence of God? Apart from anything else, the Bible contains the ongoing, unfolding narrative of God's encounter with humanity down through the ages. That narrative provides guidelines for us as we seek to notice God. The Bible also introduces us to Jesus. It is in the Bible that Jesus comes alive and is made real for us. We see God in human form, showing us what life is all about and calling us to participate with him in the emerging kingdom of God. We find ourselves as we find Jesus. But even beyond all this, the Bible can become a source of mystical encounter through which we not only hear *about* God but also hear *from* God.

One could say that the Bible is the place to start when it comes to searching for God. And indeed this has been true for many people. By reading the Bible, by accident or on purpose, they have encountered the power of God and the life-changing presence of Jesus. But it is also true that the Bible is not an easy book to engage. It is a sprawling, messy compilation of sixty-six different documents of various genres written over a long span of time in a variety of cultural contexts, all of them ancient. The part of the Bible closest to our own time was written nearly two thousand years ago. It is a challenge to create ways in which we can encounter the Bible that span the time and cultural gap and connect with our postmodern sensibilities. The Bible is a potent document that points the way for us to God as we open ourselves to it.

One could also say that the Bible is the place to go to continue to have a relationship with God. And indeed all forms of Christian spirituality include some form of biblical reflection. For those who have tasted of the Divine Presence, there is strong impetus to engage the Bible because herein one finds life and renewal.

Finally, the fact is that Christian spirituality is bound to the Bible. There is no way around it. Although different Christians give different weight to the words of Scripture, all agree that in some way the Bible is "inspired." The Bible is not merely a human composition. While it is that, it is more than that. The challenge is to discern the presence of the Other in its pages. Even more, the challenge is to open oneself to that Presence. The Bible is the primary means by which we encounter the voice of God.

6

Creation, Culture and Creativity

Laird Hamilton is arguably the greatest living big-wave surfer. By big waves we are talking about monsters that range upward from fifty feet to the true giants over one hundred feet. Hamilton is quoted as saying: "If you can look at one of these waves and you don't believe that there's something greater than we are, then you've got some serious analyzing to do and you should go sit under a tree for a very long time."[1]

Susan Casey, who quotes Hamilton in her book *The Wave*, seeks to convey from her own experience the otherworldliness of these gigantic waves:

> A wave unlike the others had arrived: a true freak. It was the result of God knows what trickster energies in the Pacific, an eagle rampaging through a parade of chickens. Instinctively I flinched as it rose into a sheer cliff, flicking the surfers off its face with casual violence. It was the biggest wave I had ever seen . . . and watching it I felt amazement and fear and humility. . . . By this point I had seen plenty of waves in the fifty-foot range, and though they were truly impressive, until now I hadn't felt the kind of awe that this wave inspired.[2]

Reading Casey's words, I am struck by her almost instinctive use of religious language to describe this extraordinary experience. Awe, wonder, beauty, fear, joy, amazement, terror, delight—these are all words we use when we come across something on this planet that astounds us. Hamilton's sense that the great waves give testimony to the reality of "something greater than we are," also speaks to the way our planet resonates with the divine.

The Creator God

God is the name we give to the creator. In creating this planet and all that is on it, God left fingerprints all over creation: in the wind and the waves, in the breathtaking beauty of a sunset, in the majesty of Mt. Hood shimmering in the early morning sun, in the complexity of a drop of water, in the annual two-thousand-mile, multigenerational migration of Monarch butterflies, and so on—you have your own examples.

Genesis, the first book of the Bible, tells the story of creation in wonderful, broad-brush pictorial language. God creates the heavens and the earth: land, sea, sky and stars. Then God creates life itself: vegetation of all sorts followed by "swarms of living creatures"—birds, "great sea monsters," "cattle and creeping things and wild animals of the earth of every kind." God sees this creation and pronounces it to be "good" (Genesis 1). Within this created world we encounter traces of the creator. The gift of creation bears the marks of the giver. The beauty we see in the created world is not God, but as the medieval world knew, "beauty is a transcendental form of God's presence, and therefore . . . experiences of beauty can be understood, by analogy, as experiences of God."[3]

St. Paul, in his letter to the Romans, observes that "the basic reality of God is plain enough. Open your eyes and there it is!

By taking a long and thoughtful look at what God has created, people have always been able to see what their eyes as such can't see: eternal power, for instance, and the mystery of his divine being" (Romans 1:20 *The Message*).

But how does this happen? What does it mean to notice God in nature by way of *analogy*? An analogy, by definition, is based on the similarity of two things, the mutual resemblance and the transferring of information regarding one to the other. By means of analogy we move from what we see and know to what we do not see and do not know. For example, by sitting in the midst of a vast, green meadow, dotted with spreading maple trees, covered with delicate flowers, alive with bee and bird, we learn about the beauty of God: If God created this tranquil paradise, God must be a great artist.

Some years ago I visited the Victoria Falls in Zimbabwe. The Victoria Falls is such an improbable phenomenon. Up-river from the falls the mile-wide Zambezi River flows along at a leisurely pace. It is a quiet, steady, forceful African river, minding its own business, when suddenly it is confronted by a great gash in the earth. It is as if someone took an ax and plunged it deep into the ground, cutting the river in two. The river, in protest and with great agitation, plunges over the side of the gash and falls hundreds of feet to the bottom of the ravine. As the river leaps across the edge of the canyon and dives down to the bottom, the water roars and boils. It sends up great clouds of mist and spray. It becomes a wild, enraged torrent before reassembling below and racing through the canyon and over the cataracts, having been reduced from a body of water one mile wide to a swift and dangerous river a few hundred yards wide.

Standing there at the edge of Victoria Falls I could not help but feel the power of water—the wild, untamable, irresistible power of water. As you peer through the mist of water, the falls are revealed then suddenly concealed, only to be revealed again in a different place, much like the way in which God's power and presence is hidden and revealed in our lives, hidden only to come at us in a new way in a new place. Such power, such a powerful God—and so the meditation unfolds.

Beauty, power, intricacy, elegance, order in creation can evoke strong emotional reactions: awe, wonder, delight, longing, deep stillness, even reverence. It is a short step from awe in response to creation to even deeper awe for the creator. In the same way that God looked out at creation and found it to be "good," so too we are called upon to take great pleasure in that creation.

Here is St. Augustine's response, crafted into a prayer:

> I set before the sight of my spirit the whole creation, whatsoever we can see therein (as sea, earth, air, stars, trees, mortal creatures): yea and whatever in it we do not see. . . . And Thee, O Lord, I imagined on every part environing and pervading it, though in every way infinite . . . so conceived I Thy creation, itself finite, yet full of Thee, the infinite: and I said, behold God and behold what God hast created.[4]

To name God as creator and to take pleasure in that creation is to see intimations of God. Our noticing can lead us to the sense that God's Spirit fills all of creation, as Augustine suggests. Here is how Elizabeth Johnson puts it:

> [R]ecall the age-old truth that the incomprehensible mystery of God lies beyond all human control and understanding. Rather than signifying divine absence, this points to *a divine overabundance that fills the world to its depths and then overflows.* There is no end to the being and fullness of God, who creates heaven and earth and is con-

> tinuously present and active throughout the world, in all ages and all cultures. Throughout history this gracious mystery approaches us with little theophanies, signs and revelations and events that invite us into relationship.[5]

It is this overabundance that we touch and tap into and that brings such delight and points to a creator. Creation is a gift to us that expresses the giver, and so we can find God in creation.

Noticing God's presence in God's work of creation is yet another way by which we can apprehend the reality of God. Gerard Manley Hopkins, the great Jesuit poet, expressed it like this:

> The world is charged with the grandeur of God.
> It will flame out, like shining from shook foil.[6]

Having said all this, I also need to note that noticing God in the wonder of creation is a rather different journey than attempting to use the creation as an argument for God's existence. That is another essay altogether. Nor is this chapter the place to wrestle with the difficult question of how a "good" creation came to contain so much sadness. I have not forgotten that all is not well on this planet. The world contains not just the grandeur of mountains, the beauty of flowers and the humor of giraffes. It also contains the nuisance of mosquitoes, the terror of tornadoes and the threat of cancer. But in spite of the reality of the destructive forces on our planet, we have the capacity to see beyond such things as war, pestilence and natural disaster. We can still sense the original glory through the fog of our distortions. But only if we are willing to open ourselves to that journey.

Noticing God in Culture

Perhaps the most amazing aspect of God's work as creator is God's creation of human beings. We are "created in the image of God" and as such bear the marks of God in us and upon us. One such mark is our ability to create. And it is in the midst of that creativity that we touch the divine. And so we stand outside in awe "under a canopy of stars," and then one of us paints "something called *The Starry Night* (Van Gogh) that gives us fresh eyes for this gift of night."[7] Culture is what we humans make of creation. Our cultural products give testimony to the reality of God when we have eyes to see and ears to hear. So it is that we turn in a God-ward direction under the power of a great symphony, through the transcendence of medieval murals in majestic European cathedrals or via the mesmerizing vision of Dante's great poem *Divine Comedy*. Our cultural products in all their creativity move us toward God.

How is it that we come to notice God in culture? William Dyrness puts it this way: "Because of the way the world is made and God's continued presence in that world, and because human agents are made in the image of God, cultural products, when they are good and true, can move people toward God."[8] So when a poet puts to verse her encounter with creation, she is expressing for all of us what she has experienced. And as we read her poem, we too are moved to new understanding and even to a new apprehension of divine presence. So Andrew Greeley contends that culture "is a '*locus theologicus*,' a theological place—the locale in which one may encounter God."[9] But then we must ask, *Where* is God in the music, the film and the painting? Where is God in the dance, the sculpture, the poem or any of the other forms of artistic expression?

My friends and colleagues Craig Detweiler and Barry Taylor have an interesting take on popular culture in their book *A Matrix of Meanings: Finding God in Pop Culture*. While they rec- [illegible] the delusions and destruction one can find in pop [illegible] they also see a positive side. Noticing that so many people, especially younger people, are captivated by pop culture, they examine: "where God might be lurking in the songs, shows, and films kids continually return to for solace and meaning. . . . We turn to pop culture in our efforts to understand God and to recognize the twenty-first-century face of Jesus."[10]

Detweiler and Taylor argue that in the same way that God speaks through "unlikely means [such] as a burning bush, a donkey, and a dream" and that Jesus chooses dishonest tax collectors and unschooled fishermen to initiate his kingdom, so too God speaks through pop culture today. They identify films such as *The Apostle, Dead Man Walking* and *Magnolia,* as well as television shows like *The Simpsons* and *The West Wing,* as examples of how God's truth finds expression in unlikely places.[11] More recent examples might be films like the *Lord of the Rings* trilogy and the *Narnia* series and TV shows like *Joan of Arcadia.* Or take the *Star Trek* films, which raise a host of religious questions. The first film poses the whole issue of what makes one human; V'ger has no soul and therefore his existence has no purpose. *Star Trek II* has the Genesis project. In the third film Spock is resurrected, while the focus of film four is how to be good stewards of the earth (save the whales). Then number five involves a search for God at the edges of the universe. Here is much rich material to ponder and discuss!

How do movies and TV shows reveal the Divine? I think there are several answers to this question.

Clearly films and other cultural artifacts, as I have suggested, have the power to generate conversation about religious matters. Take, for example, the conversation sparked by 1999 sci-fi film *The Matrix,* which touched the imagination of a whole generation. Hundreds of websites were spawned as people asked "Was Neo the One?" and what this might mean for life as we know it. Do we live in the midst of an artificially generated dream designed to keep us content as life is sucked out of us? Is this what modern advertising is all about? What does it mean to be human in a broken world? What "red pill/blue pill" choice are we called upon to make? These were religious questions framed by the film in religious language and images. And it is not just *The Matrix*. Given the prevalence of religious themes in film today, opportunities for discussing important issues abound.

Film also provides the "primary stories around which we shape our lives. . . . Movies function as a primary source of power and meaning for people throughout the world," writes theologian and film critic Robert Johnston.[12] We are powerfully shaped by the stories we embrace from film. They teach us about life, meaning, relationships, values, behavior, God and many other things. Films inspire us (*The Shawshank Redemption*). Films warn us (*Dr. Strangelove*). Films reveal God to us in new ways (*The Lord of the Rings*). Films bring us hope (*It's a Wonderful Life*). The list could go on.

William Dyrness discusses the research of Clive Marsh concerning the experience of people going to movies. Marsh

> found that though people often say they go to a movie to "escape," in fact "they often get more than they expect." His study leads him to conclude that going to movies, and entertainment more generally, "is taking the place of religion as a cultural site where the task of meaning-making is undertaken." Going to movies and other kinds of entertainment becomes part of the way that people make something of their lives.[13]

Some films tackle religious themes directly. A variety of Jesus films do so, for example, ranging from lavish Hollywood productions like Cecil B. DeMille's *The King of Kings* (1927) and George Stevens's *The Greatest Story Ever Told* (1965) to musical adaptations like *Godspell* and *Jesus Christ Superstar* (both 1973). Many say that Franco Zeffirelli's six-and-a-half-hour-long *Jesus of Nazareth* (1977) is the best Jesus film ever. There are also those films that tell the Jesus story from odd points of view, such as Martin Scorsese's *The Last Temptation of Christ* (1988), *Jesus of Montreal* (1989) and Monty Python's *Life of Brian* (1979). The challenge with such films, of course, is to distinguish between fact and fancy. This challenge can engage us in reading and conversation that deepens our spiritual understanding.

But film does even more than all this. We can encounter the presence of God in the film itself. My colleague Rob Johnston went to see *Becket*, and there in the theater heard God call him to ministry. Moments of grace can come even in films that one would never expect to evoke spiritual experience. Greg Garrett talks about his experience of the Quentin Tarantino film *Pulp Fiction:* "What I took away from *Pulp Fiction* was not the violent action, dark humor, and crudity, but embedded themes of grace and redemption and the belief that God was real and powerful. For me, *Pulp Fiction* was a deeply spiritual film."[14] Craig Detweiler's spiritual journey began with Martin Scorsese's *Raging Bull*. "Something was revealed to me through *Raging Bull*—a sense of longing, need, and desperation. . . . God chose to use a profane movie to reveal blinding truth to my parched and weary soul; the Spirit spoke through the big screen."[15] As Detweiler puts it, "The same God who spoke through dreams and visions in the Bible is still communicating through our celluloid dreams—the movies."[16]

The power of film using story, metaphor, sight and sound can open us to noticing God in new and surprising ways.

Music is a sublime form of human creativity. For many of us, music is "God's language" in which we notice God most easily. In the episode "Fat Chance" of the PBS show *Inspector Morse*,

Morse is in conversation with a woman who happens to be an Anglican priest. It is a quiet conversation. They are alone, sitting on his veranda sipping wine. Morse asks about her "conversion," how she got involved with the whole God thing. After she explains she asks Morse about his view of God. Cynical Morse, ever the pragmatic detective, has little to say except, "Sometimes, when I am listening to music . . ." He leaves it at that, but the viewers know that if Morse is ever to encounter God it will be via the classical music he loves so much.

Music touches us in profound ways. Take, for example, the power of the music of Bruce Springsteen.[17] My son-in-law, Joe Tito, is a great Bruce Springsteen fan. It is not uncommon to arrive at his house and hear Bruce singing loudly in the kitchen while Joe cooks. Joe is a member of the "Church of Bruce." Joe is not alone in his devotion to Bruce. Linda Randall, in her book about Springsteen (*Finding Grace in the Concert Hall: Community & Meaning Among Springsteen Fans*), charts the dimensions of the worldwide community of Bruce fans. She, herself, is a fan:

> I am someone who has never adjusted to organized religion, but who longs for something to believe in, something to provide a little warmth on those cold nights of the soul, and some "reason to believe." Springsteen has provided illumination for me and for many of his faithful fans in the form of joy, and I am thankful for this. Joy may be the emotion that brings us closest to the holy.[18]

She goes on to talk about her experience at a Springsteen concert in Albany, New York: "This proved to be a terrific and transforming experience for me. . . . My response was completely visceral, emotional, nonintellectual, and absolutely unexplainable in the moment. I felt in unison, with all those around me and with myself. . . . To feel a part . . . of this joyous, raucous celebration of life, love, friendship, and music was an *extra*ordinary encounter. I experienced transcendence, inclusion, redemption, and felt a part of the performance. I felt the grace of the universe."[19] Speaking of a concert in Charlotte, North Carolina, she sums up her experience: "Only one other 'public' experience in my life even came close to resembling my Springsteen experience and that was a Billy Graham crusade I'd attended as a young teen. Springsteen's music and words spoke to me, to some inner longing, as much as Billy Graham's words had some 40 years earlier, and this was both intriguing and mystifying."[20]

Springsteen's music has the power to help us notice God—lyrics, sound, setting all combined to touch us profoundly.[21] A powerful piece of music resonates with something deep within us. There is a connection. Spirit speaks to spirit.

Our vast corpus of religious music testifies to transcendence. God inspires music. For those who create music, who perform music and who listen to music, music can become a means of noticing God, a means of worshiping God, as well as an attempt to express one's experience of God.

Another art form in which one can catches glimpses of God is the vast world of literature. This world is too large to do more than touch on, but perhaps three examples will illustrate how the written word can help us notice God's presence in the world.

Take, for example, this reflection in Alexander McCall Smith's book *The Charming Quirks of Others*. Isabel Dalhousie, the main character, is "a moral philosopher by trade."[22] She publishes a professional journal: *Review of Applied Ethics*. Isabel is not a religious person, but in reviewing a paper sent for publication, she muses:

> Perhaps there was a force of moral goodness, every bit as powerful, in its way, as any of the physical forces that kept electrons in circulation about the nucleus of an atom. Perhaps we understood that, even if we acted against it, even if we denied it. And that force could be called anything, God being one name that people gave to it. And we knew that it was there because we felt its presence, as the religious believer may be convinced in his very bones of the presence of God, even if we could not describe the nature of it.
>
> . . . She thought she had come to some understanding of goodness, but it had been illusory, a quick-silver flash of vision, nothing more. Perhaps this is how goodness—or God—visited us: so quickly and without warning that we might easily miss it, but perceptible none the less, and transforming beyond the transformative power of anything else we have known.[23]

This is an interesting reflection on the nature of moral law, on morality itself, on the nature and origin of conscience, as well as the power of epiphanies. As such it describes yet another way God might be noticed in this world. Such a description has the power to cause us to reflect on our own experience and perhaps to understand it better and to notice what we might not have noticed otherwise. We become more conscious. We see in new ways.

John Updike is another author who has explored the question of God in various ways in his vast corpus of literature. In his novel *Roger's Version,* a young computer programmer, Dale Kohler, argues that the existence of God can be demonstrated by the physics of the big bang theory. Dale lays out his case to Roger Lambert, a professor at Harvard Divinity School. "Everywhere you look . . . there are these terrifically finely adjusted constants that have to be just what they are, or there wouldn't be a world we could recognize, and there's no intrinsic reason for those constants to be what they are except to say *God made them that way.* God made heaven and Earth. It's what science has come to. Believe me."[24]

Interestingly, Roger, the professor of theology, is offended by this search for God by means of mathematics, preferring Barth's view of God as *totally other.* He responds to Dale:

> For myself, I must confess I find your whole idea aesthetically and ethically repulsive. Aesthetically because it describes a God Who lets Himself be intellectually trapped and ethically because it eliminates faith from religion, it takes away our freedom to believe or doubt. A God you could prove makes the whole thing immensely, oh, uninteresting. Pat. Whatever else God may be He shouldn't be pat.[25]

And so we are drawn to the whole question of the search for God by means of scientific proof and intellectual argument—and to the challenges of such an approach.

Poets in particular unlock reality for us. A current favorite of mine is Billy Collins, the former Poet Laureate of America. In his poem "The Dead" he talks about how the dead look down on us through glass-bottom boats while rowing "slowly through eternity."[26] In this amusing, homey, profound poem, Collins raises questions of life and death and life after death. Who has not been moved at some point by a poem, even by a turn of phrase, that unlocks a new reality for us? Surely poetry alone is capable of nurturing our search for God and opening our eyes to transcendence.

Much more could be said about how the artifacts of culture reveal the presence of God amongst us and in us. I have said nothing about painting, sculpture or dance—nor about theater, television or fashion. The same argument can be made in each of these creative spheres. Each pushes us in some way beyond ourselves when we have eyes to see. Each moves us to a deeper understanding of ourselves, of our place in the world and in human society, and of what lies beyond and beneath our shared reality. It is the power of human imagination which uses these means to plumb the mystery and the glory of the created world in which we live, filled as it is with God.

The Creative Process

If it is true that our encounters with art provide us with innumerable opportunities for noticing God, then we should not be surprised to discover that the act of creation itself is often spoken of as such an opportunity. Our artists have much to teach us about noticing God.

Robert Wuthnow, the eminent Princeton University sociologist, talks about the connection between art and spirituality in his book *Creative Spirituality: The Way of the Artist.* In interviews with hundreds of artists, he finds that many of them seek to provide in their art "small experiences of transcendence that in themselves become reasons for hope." Wuthnow goes on: "It is the creative process itself that momentarily transcends time, offering an awareness that something other than the ordinary can exist and, through that existence, reinvigorate the flawed aspirations of ordinary people."[27]

There are times when the very creation of art leads to a mystical experience. Bob McGovern talks about working on a wood sculpture "when ordinary time and space seemed to disappear and spiritual light emanated from the object. 'I think you have to be deaf, dumb, and blind not to realize that when you work with a creation you are dealing with something that's bigger and wrapped in the cosmos.' "[28] Wuthnow quotes a painter who says that "there are some times when I don't know where that energy is coming from. The brush leads me and it seems to have nothing to do with my body. It is coming purely from the spirit. It's a very special feeling when I do this. There's a oneness with the sacred, with the divine."[29]

Such reports are not surprising. We are created in the image of God and creativity is a prime characteristic of God. This chapter has been discussing the wonder of God's creative activity. We too have been given the ability to create. We can weave together various elements to produce something unique, something that sparkles with truth and reality. What artists seek to capture is not just something within themselves but also "something beyond, hovering on the edges of their imaginations, drawing them out."[30] In the creative process we access God on some level. We touch the Mystery and then we express in various art forms what we encounter in God. God inspires the creativity. In the creative process we are touching God in us and around us.

Thus art is a response to God; it is praise of God; it is an offering to God; it is teaching about God; it is the fruit of listening to God; it is a celebration of God. "If God is truly majestic and transcendent, some responses to this realization may defy expression in anything but imaginative lyrics and images."[31]

What does art do to us? Wuthnow cites a study in which 32 percent of the people attending a musical performance said they had experienced "a strong sense of being in the presence of something sacred." Others say they are "inspired" in mind and spirit through art. Still others say the arts influenced their spiritual development.[32] How does this happen? In paying attention to an artist's work do we experience some of the same Spirit that inspired the artist? Or does the artifact witness to the Divine or even contain a touch of the Divine? Or is it that the music or painting resonates with a deep part of ourselves (our spirit)? Maybe all are true. How art connects with us is mysterious and often beyond the rational. But the record shows that such encounters do occur.

Significance

Can we explain *how* we encounter God in nature, art and creativity? The paths vary. There is *the way of analogy*. We see in nature a striking phenomenon—power, beauty, design—and it brings to us an awareness of what (or who) lies behind such wonders. There is *the way of affect*. We are struck with awe over the beauty of the Grand Canyon. Or we find ourselves weeping, inexplicably, as we listen to great music that brings to the surface deep feelings in us, feelings that resonate with God.

There is *the way of the intellect* as we seek to probe the deeper mysteries of creation and in so doing bump up against the Creator. There is also *the way of the artist* in which the very act of creation puts us in touch with Spirit, so that both artist and viewer are moved beyond themselves.

I think Elizabeth Johnson describes well this "sense of God" in our culture at this point in time: "Since the middle of the twentieth century, a burgeoning renaissance of insight into God has been taking place." She goes on:

> People have perceived this sacred presence disclosing itself in the most diverse ways: in nature; in historical events; in art, music, and dance; in interior peacefulness and exterior healing; in the whole range of human experiences both good and bad, particularly love and loss. They have sensed it when they meet limits, the uncanny, the surprising, an unusual fullness or emptiness of life, and have sought union

> through a vast variety of practices. . . . People are discovering God again not in the sense of deducing abstract notions but in the sense of encountering the divine presence and absence in their everyday experiences of struggle and hope, both ordinary and extraordinary.[33]

We encounter myriad intimations of transcendence—of God—in our daily lives if we take the time and give the attention needed to be present in our observing. When we do, we learn to see that which is there, that which people down through the ages have called God. The medieval German mystic Meister Eckhart expresses it well in his poem "Apprehend God":

> Apprehend God in all things,
> for God is in all things.
>
> Every single creature is full of God
> and is a book about God.
>
> Every creature is a word of God.
> If I spent enough time with the tiniest creature—
> even a caterpillar—
> I would never have to prepare a sermon.
> So full of God is every creature.[34]

7

Church

Some may ask why have I waited until the final chapter to talk about church. Isn't church attendance at the very heart of Christian spirituality?

The fact is that many people today resist the idea of attending church—and with good reason. In their minds, a sharp divide exists between spirituality and religion. *Spirituality,* which is seen as both fascinating and attractive, is understood to be good—whereas *religion,* which is thought to reek of rules and regulations, institutions, hierarchy and lifelessness, is seen as irrelevant at the best and destructive at the worst. Religion is equated to church and church is equated to dead rituals, boring services, judgmental pronouncements, superficial emotion and constricted living. Who wants that? People are looking for God. They don't want all the negativity.

Religion is thought to get in the way of spirituality. Church is understood to be an impediment to true faith. For example, one of the complaints of the so-called Millennial generation[1] is that they tried church and it proved to be flawed. This is the generation that, as high school students, was active in church and in church-based organizations. These were the WWJD crowd ("What Would Jesus Do?") and the kids who prayed around the flagpole at high school early in the morning. The Millennials were the ones who used to chastise their parents and Gen-X siblings for not going to church. However, once the Millennials reached college age, their views began to change. They left church in droves, claiming that church was, of all things, "*unChristian*." This is the title of David Kinnaman's book that charts this generational movement from enthusiastic church adherents to scathing church critics.[2]

UnChristian lists seven specific complaints against the church.[3] This is not the place to discuss these criticisms, many of which are valid complaints. But I want to suggest that while these indictments of organized religion have truth to them, it is virtually impossible on one's own to explore, much less to live out faithfully, the Way of Jesus. We need others both to find and to follow God—and this implies some sort of community involvement. We need the stories of others to point the way. We need the wisdom of others as we seek to understand our own stories. We need others to join with us as we explore the God-question. We need others as we seek to reach out to God. We need others to nurture the seeds of newly emerging faith. In other words, we need a context within which to pursue spirituality.

The particular kind of community we need will vary from person to person. For some, the traditional church still works, especially if it is filled with loving folk. For others, one of the emerging churches makes more sense with its ongoing experiments in what it means to be a community of faith. Still others find that the liturgical church, rooted in ancient forms of Christianity, brings life and sustenance to them. Maybe for some the operative "fellowship" (that ancient Christian name for groups of Jesus followers) will be a small group meeting weekly in someone's home.

We have been promised that when we gather together in the name of God, God shows up too. Part of this truth is that in such situations we simply are more alert to the presence of God. We come to worship God and so we open ourselves to God. But the reality of God's presence also has to do with the promise of Jesus that "where two or three are gathered in my name, I am there among them" (Matthew 18:20).

When the church is being what it is meant to be, any of these communities can provide a rich and powerful environment for God-encounters. While the structures and practices of the communities may take different forms, they share certain key features such as worship, sacraments and teaching, which deserve our attention.

Worship

Worship is certainly the place where "two or three are gathered" in the name of Jesus. What happens here? How is God's presence manifest? Where should we look and how do we respond? What are the elements of Christian worship, and how does each reveal God?

First there is the *music*. Almost all Christian worship services contain music, sometimes lots of music. There may be hymns to sing, a choir to listen to, solos, an organ (or a band) to focus our meditation. In certain churches bells are rung at special places in the service. Right from the very beginning of Judeo-Christian worship, those who gathered in the name of God did so in the context of music. The ancient Psalms collected together in the Old Testament were often sung or chanted. Certain New Testament passages include snatches of songs that were sung by the first Christians. Early witnesses give evidence that as worship evolved in the newly forming church, music was part of the process.

Why music? In the previous chapter I discussed the power of music to open us to the presence of God. I talked about how the experience of music in the context of community has great power to move our souls deeply, to lift our hearts to the Other and to reveal truth to us. The very God who inspires the creation of the music in the first place stands behind that music as it is performed. And at times we can sense God's presence as we let ourselves rest in the music, as it explores and reveals transcendence and mystery.

I remember how music moved me during the period following my father's death. At such moments we are more sensitive to things of the Spirit. It is as if we are tuned into transcendence in a deeper way at transitional moments. Hearing "Ode to Joy" invariably brought me to tears. There was a deep resonance with the "Joy" that transcends death. Through the vehicle of Beethoven's great composition it felt as if I had touched Joy and was touched by Joy.

Then there is the *sermon*. Sermons have a mixed reputation because so many of them are dull, uninspiring, trite or meandering. Lots of bad sermons get preached each year. But then there are the others, the ones that penetrate our hearts, move our minds and free our souls. A gifted speaker delivering a God-inspired message, moves us to new places in our search for God. Sermons can be signposts pointing us to God. They provide rich information about the ways of God on this planet, the call of God to each of us and the joy of following the Way that leads to wholeness. What is more, at their best, sermons communicate the very presence and voice of God. (More about sermons when I get to the teaching ministry of the church.)

I have heard more sermons over the years than I could count. They ranged from the truly awful to the eminently forgettable to the mildly interesting to the momentarily challenging to the genuinely moving and life-changing. During the past decade I was privileged to sit under the ministry of (the now retired) Rev. Hartshorn Murphy at St. Augustine's by-the-Sea Episcopal Church in Santa Monica, California. Week after week he brought alive the Gospel passage for the day. I was moved. I was enlightened. I was amused. I was challenged. Only rarely was I uninterested. Taken together, his sermons took me to a new place in my Christian understanding and activity. Sermons are like that. Sometimes it is an individual sermon that produces an "aha" moment: "Oh, so that is what it is all about." But generally it is when we listen to a series of sermons over time that we are moved to open ourselves—if we have ears to hear.

I have preached a number of sermons over the years, and I suspect that these sermons ranged from the truly awful (I apologize; I was just a teenager trying my best!) to the forgettable to, on occasion, genuinely moving sermons. Curiously, at times what was "heard" was not really my main point but something in the sermon that resonated with a particular person. It was almost as if there was a Voice behind my voice. The experience of preaching includes moments when I felt I was a mere voice for that Voice.

The reading of the *Scripture* on which the sermon focuses is an important part of the worship service. Some of the best sermons are those that unlock the meaning of the Bible and connect it to the lives of the congregation. The text all by itself has the power to move us. In a previous chapter I talked about how the Bible reveals God. The reading of the Bible as part of worship can create sacred space within which the Bible comes alive for us.

Prayer is a central feature of Christian worship. In this element of the service we make a conscious and deliberate attempt to reach out to God. By means of the recitation of ancient words—prayers echoed over and over again down through the centuries—we open our hearts to the living presence of God. By means of spontaneous expressions of prayer—filled with joy or suffering, worry or fear, concern or longing, hope, love and wonder—we join together to affirm our deep belief (and experience) that God hears, values and answers our prayers. In the midst of prayer there is Presence.

Worship also includes the *sacraments*, such as Communion, baptism, weddings and funerals—each of which points to a greater reality. A sacrament is defined as an external sign of an inward grace, which is the theological way of saying that such rites reveal the presence of God in an immediate way. I want to treat sacraments separately since they have been understood through the centuries to be special moments when the presence of God is especially palpable. Not that God is not present or only faintly present in other parts of the service; it is just that the sacraments, such as Communion, have an intensity that reveals God. Some would go so far as to say that the rite actually confers grace—a visible form of an invisible grace.[4]

While worship in all its elements can reveal God powerfully, so too worship can be nothing more than dull repetition—a faint echo of what once was powerful. Music can become sentimental and superficial. Sermons can be dull, uninformative or even inaccurate. Prayer gets lost in archaic language, sentimental affect, inauthentic words and mere repetition. Sacraments become simply rites that have lost the meaning behind them. All this conspires together to deaden our sense of Presence. When worship becomes routinized, it loses its power to draw us God-ward. Still, even in the midst of a dull, ponderous and pathetic version of worship, it is possible to encounter God because the character of God is always to be present. Bad worship makes it difficult to notice God's presence; good worship opens avenues of encounter.

In order for us to notice God in the midst of worship, we are required to be fully present in the midst of Presence. We need to sing, to say, to listen, to respond, to hear, to ponder, to pray, to participate, to give, to receive, to grieve, to rejoice fully—and so open ourselves to the Presence we have gathered to praise.

Sacraments

Sacraments reveal God.

Why do these ancient rites, performed over and over again down through the centuries, seem to have such power for us? Part of the reason has to do with the sacredness of the ceremony. A wedding, a baptism, a funeral—these are all seminal events that signify transition: beginnings and endings, new options and new challenges. These rites mark out for us turning points in our lives and so they become definitional for us.

But there is something else about these sacraments. They link us to the sacred.

Take baptism. Baptism is a re-creation of the death and resurrection of Jesus. As we go under the water (either literally in pond or pool or symbolically with sprinkled water), so we reenact the death of Jesus. As we rise up out of the water, so we reenact the resurrection of Jesus. Through baptism we experience a symbolic connection to Jesus, the one to whom we pledge allegiance via this act. But theology tells us that baptism is more than mere symbol. We become one with Christ: Christ in us. We have touched a mystery and we are changed.[5]

Or take the sacrament of marriage. The Episcopal service begins: "Dearly beloved: We have come together in the presence of God to witness and bless the joining together of this man and this woman in Holy Matrimony."[6] The community is gathered in the presence of God in this special place at this special time to give witness to the vows given and received, which proclaim a new beginning. Something important is taking place, something that touches on divine reality and divine presence—and we are moved. What was it about the recent royal wedding between Prince William and Catherine Middleton that not only drew three billion viewers worldwide but deeply moved those who watched via television? Certainly the pomp and circumstance along with all the elegance, choreography, costumes and history were all part of the appeal. But it was also the power of the ceremony in all its simplicity with its ancient and rich language that bespoke powerful realities into which this young couple willingly moved. It was the Reality behind that moment that touched us and reminded us again that we live in a world filled with Presence.

Or take the rite of burial: "Into your hands, O merciful Savior, we commend your servant [Name]. . . . Receive *him/her* into the arms of your mercy, into the blessed rest of everlasting peace, and into the glorious company of the saints in light."[7] What powerful hope lies behind these words—hope of resurrection, hope of new life, hope of eternal life, hope that stands over against our darkest fear that death is termination. The sacrament of burial declares that this present reality in which we now live is mere precursor to a new, vital reality where God is fully present (call it heaven, eternal life, whatever). Death is a door not an ending. In the ringing words of this service we confront true Reality in its fullest form: "I am Resurrection and I am Life, says the Lord. Whoever has faith in me shall have life, even though he die. . . . As for me, I know that my Redeemer lives and that at the last he will stand upon the earth. After my awaking, he will raise me up; and in my body I shall see God. I myself shall see, and my eyes behold him who is my friend and not a stranger."[8]

It is the mystery behind the sacrament that gives power to the moment, and we touch that Presence as we celebrate the sacrament.

The sacrament that interests me most is the Eucharist (Communion, the Lord's Supper—all names for the same act) because at the very heart of the Eucharist is an encounter with Jesus. Jesus himself implemented this sacrament. As his death drew near, in the context of a traditional Jewish Passover celebration, he took two common substances—bread and wine—and gave them new meaning. He took the bread and said, "This is my body which is given for you." He took the wine and said, "This is my blood of the new covenant, which is shed for you and for many for the forgiveness of sins."[9]

Jesus said, "Do this in remembrance of me." So we remember, over and over again, the power and presence of Jesus.[10] Bread as body, wine as blood—elements that help us remember and that bring us into intimate contact with Jesus. No matter how one interprets this ritual (literally, figuratively, symbolically), in it we contact Jesus in a visible, tactile way. We consume the bread and wine. We take Jesus into ourselves. In this act there is a presence—an external sign of something sacred taking place in and amongst us. It is not just that memory is evoked; grace is imparted. Here is mystery. Here is divine/human contact.

In the act of Communion, as we remember what has been done on our behalf by the death and resurrection of Jesus and thus remember who Jesus is, so we connect again the two worlds within which we live: the world of spirit and the world of flesh. Our balance is righted, as it were, and after the worship service we go out again into the ever-present, ever-demanding world of daily life with a renewed peace and with a sense of Presence—when this sacrament becomes the grace it is for us. Listen to Mother Teresa of Calcutta:

> My great love is Jesus in the Eucharist, in Holy Communion. There I meet him, I receive him, I love him; then I rediscover him and serve him in the poorest of the poor. . . . Only with assiduous prayer and with Communion are we able to live with Jesus and for Jesus with our poor and for our poor and needy.[11]

Men and women have encountered Sacred Presence via the sacraments—strongly powerful experiences. Not always, maybe not even usually, but sometimes in the midst of the sacrament the presence of God is palpable.

Teaching

We come to understand the nature of worship, the sacraments, the Bible and other aspects of Christian life via the teaching ministry of the church. Information is important in our search for spiritual truth. Our minds need to be fully engaged. We have seen the role the Bible plays in Christian understanding of truth (in chapter five). Here I focus on how such Christian understanding is communicated and how we can engage with that process in helpful ways.

Sermons are probably the primary way by which we learn about Christian truth. The sermon has become the centerpiece of the worship in many churches. Yet when you think about it, a sermon is an anomaly in our culture. Where else do people gather and listen to a weekly lecture/exposition? Mostly we get information from TV that comes to us in the form of short monologues that range from informed comment to rant. So a home-crafted homily by a local minister drawn from an ancient text and connected to ordinary life seems like something from a different era. Yet the crowds still gather in great numbers for such sermons, as the megachurches demonstrate each week. We seem to yearn for wisdom beyond our cultural confines.

At its best, a sermon taps into ancient wisdom. One goal of a good sermon is to reveal what Scripture is saying and then to make connections between these ideas and our personal stories. The best sermons sparkle with God-driven reality. "This is the way things are. This is who God is. This is how we are meant to live." And so the tradition lives on in us and among us. Sermons can reveal God.

The teaching ministry of the church also takes place in settings other than the Sunday service. While it is a struggle to find time-slots that allow people to gather for what used to be called "Christian education," the church has been inventive in how it undertakes this ministry. Men's groups gather for breakfast before work. Women's groups gather for dinner and conversation at a local restaurant. Youth groups go to camps for fun and games and serious conversation. Couples meet weekly in each other's homes for Bible study. Book groups flourish. Church-based websites point people to links that provide all sorts of insights. Each format has the same goal: to learn about God.

My wife and I had a weekly Bible study in our home for many years. Each week a diverse group of people would gather. We would study a particular passage from the Bible. Each week, we tried to figure out what the Bible was saying and what it all meant. We tried to figure out how the people for whom this was originally written understood what Jesus, John or Paul was saying. Then we tried to apply it. What does this ancient text say to us here and now? We slowly learned and grew and changed. It was the quality of the conversation as well as the deepening bonds of community that drew us together each week in this intentional small group.

Christianity is blessed with a long tradition of thoughtful

reflection, given shape and form in a vast corpus of writing. We have much to explore when it comes to seeking out God.

Community

All this—worship, sacraments, teaching—individual communities enact weekly all over this planet. People gather together to seek God, to learn about God, to praise God, to follow God and to seek to be God's people together in a particular place at a particular time. The heart of these communities centers on what the Bible calls *fellowship.* Fellowship is all about being together, caring for one another as well as caring for others, all the while trying to be open to and responsive to the presence of God. Community life itself can be very powerful as people seek to follow the Great Commandment given the church by Jesus: "you shall love the Lord your God with all your heart, and with all your soul, and with all your mind and with all your strength. . . . You shall love your neighbor as yourself" (Mark 12:30-31). Genuinely loving communities are very attractive. Being part of such a community changes us. But communities can become ingrown and isolated, judgmental and off-putting, dead and lifeless—a mere caricature of what they are called to be. However, when one meets the real thing, it is powerful.

What is it about fellowship that reveals God to us? I think mainly we meet God through relationships. When we know ourselves to be loved by God, we are released to love others. We are cared for so we can care for others. We are blessed so we bless others. Knowing ourselves to be loved, we can be easier on ourselves and on others. We can relax into that love. We can work on what ails us, what impedes us, what binds us, doing all this in the context of a community in which we are all striving to be better. We can learn to live with our own and others' idiosyncrasies. We get inspired to get out of ourselves and be there for others. As we laugh together and cry together and face pain together we grow together. We hold each other up. We help each other out. And we keep turning to God together to know the love that binds us together. Such a community is a good place to be. God is alive there.

Spiritual Disciplines and Practices

Such Christian communities are shaped by the spiritual disciplines and the spiritual practices in which they engage. It is in the midst of these disciplines and practices that we can and do meet God. These disciplines and practices seek to align us with the Way of Jesus and open us to the presence of God. Engaging in disciplines and practices is appropriate for all who are hungry for God no matter where they are on their spiritual journey. So for the spiritually curious, this is a good place to start. Explore the Bible, pray, go on retreat, work at the soup kitchen, join a small group. See what happens.

By *spiritual disciplines* I mean those activities undertaken in order to open oneself to the presence of God and to learn to live as a disciple of Jesus. Worship, prayer and Bible study are the primary disciplines. But other disciples such as silence and solitude help us notice the presence of God, and by journaling we chronicle and capture the unfolding of our spiritual journey. For some the discipline of simplicity enables them to escape the clutches of the materialism that chokes off their spiritual pursuit. The spiritual discipline of pilgrimage is being rediscovered—visiting those special places that seem filled with a sense of God, such as Jerusalem, Rome and Assisi. These are but a few of the intentional activities in which we can engage so as to grow our spiritual sensitivities.

You don't have to be a card-carrying church member to find great benefit in these spiritual disciplines. The very practice of a spiritual discipline opens up the reality of God to us.

For example, take the spiritual discipline of spiritual autobiography. Each of us has a spiritual autobiography whether we know it or not. We have all been created in the image of God, so God has been and is present in our lives. The problem is that we don't always notice. To stop and remember such things as our encounters with mystery, our conversations with spiritually oriented people, our involvement with a high school youth group, our prayers in the dead of night when we were fearful, our brushes with joy, our experience of love is to uncover our spiritual autobiography. The sheer process of assembling the story of one's spiritual journey brings great insight. Even better is sharing this story with others in the context of a small group gathered for the purpose of writing and then telling such stories to one another.[12]

By *spiritual practices* I mean those activities that we engage in by dint of being members of Christian communities.[13] This is what we do as followers of Jesus.[14] We worship together. We engage in issues of justice. We study the Bible. We seek to live in accord with the ethic of Jesus. Spiritual practices include such things as hospitality, service, truth-telling, almsgiving, justice, reconciliation, Sabbath-keeping, testimony, forgiveness, works of mercy, sharing and so on. Each can be a vehicle that expresses the reality of God.

Hospitality sits at the very heart of Christian community. At our best we seek to express a generous hospitality not only to those who are part of our community but to the stranger, to the person in need and to those who are disadvantaged. Such hospitality is welcoming, open and warm. It is expressed by sharing food, time and goods. It draws people together. It creates safe spaces. It welcomes the searching and the lost. When we offer hospitality we affirm the worth and humanity of others. This is especially important for those who receive little or no respect in the eyes of others. Such acts of hospitality point beyond ourselves to God who is portrayed in Scripture as the gracious host who welcomes us. Knowing God's hospitality ourselves, we are able to welcome others in God's name. In the midst of such hospitality one can encounter the presence of God.[15]

In the *spiritual practice of service or mission* the church reaches out to others in practical ways as it seeks to love others by rehabbing houses in New Orleans, by preparing and serving food at a teen drop-in center, or by organizing the Fourth of July celebration for the town. Down through the centuries churches have engaged in all manner and means of service—building schools and hospitals, putting pressure on governments to create just structures, exposing corruption in corporations, and many other prophetic acts—often at great risk. Nor should we forget that many Christian communities are deeply enriched by innumerable small acts of service performed by individual members.

Not only are such outreach programs valuable in what they give to others, they have a great impact on those who participate in them. For example, the church to which I belong in Massachusetts (Wenham First Congregational Church) goes on a mission trip every other year. They have gone to such places as the Kayenta Navajo Reservation (2006) and twice to the Christian Appalachian Project (2008, 2010). These intergenerational groups consist of an equal number of adults and kids. Kids and adults who hardly knew each another before the trip form wonderful bonds together. The Rev. Mike Duda recalls, "I remember watching a 70-year-old and a 17-year-old sitting together at dinner talking about soffits—days before the 17-year-old didn't even know what they were, yet they had struggled together to rebuild them on a dilapidated house in the Appalachian Mountains. On one trip as we gathered around a campfire in the mountains and shared the high points of our experience, a young man stood up and described how for the first time in his life he had seen his father as a man, a separate individual and not just his dad, and how he was inspired by what a compassionate, caring person he was (his dad wasn't the only one with tears in his eyes)."[16]

Sometimes it is by participating in acts of service as part of a community that we discover spiritual reality. We are part of something bigger than ourselves, something that draws on our gifts and skills, something that satisfies our longings to give to others.

Other Christian practices reveal the core of Jesus' teaching: *truth-telling* in situations where such truth brings pain to oneself; *almsgiving,* which is the old word for sharing one's wealth and possessions with others; *reconciliation* in which we seek to bring together parties in conflict; *Sabbath-keeping* by which we accept the gift of rest and reflection in a world that is constantly on the go; *testimony* in which we share our stories of faith in the midst of our successes and failures; *forgiveness* offered when forgiveness is hard; *mercy* when what we crave is revenge; *sharing* instead of hoarding. In all these ways and many more we seek to become better, more than we would otherwise be, kinder, gentler, more loving—which is what Jesus calls us to be.

A *retreat* is a rich environment in which to explore spiritual disciplines and engage in spiritual practices. There is something quite powerful about being away for a weekend with others for the purpose of opening ourselves to God. There in the quiet of a monastery, in the context of the liturgy of the hours, alone in a small room or walking the lovely grounds, we have the rare chance to be still, to focus, to listen, to seek and to touch that Presence we long for. In my own experience, silent retreats are among the most powerful environments within which to seek and know God.

Not all retreats focus on silence. Some are given over to teaching: in-depth exploration of worthy topics that touch the mysteries of life. Such retreats often revolve around lectures and discussions led by knowledgeable individuals who have something to teach us. When small group discussion is added to the mix, the impact can be quite powerful. Reflection on important issues in the context of the fellowship of others can open our eyes to new realities.

In the end, the church is all about the people. It is not about the pastor or about the building or about the program. The identity of a particular church is found in the character of the people who are formed by the community. Who are they becoming? How are they being shaped? How do they seek to follow the Way of Jesus? In what ways do they live out the presence of God? These are crucial questions. We can see the impact of God in the lives of those who seek God.

Fellowship is all about being together as people who are trying to follow the Way of Jesus. It is about being connected together. It is about love in action. When all this comes together something quite wonderful happens. A community of disparate people with quite different backgrounds, experiences and issues become a community of love and caring—the kind of community where we wish to be because we are accepted as we are. There we are engaged in the kind of worship that opens up the spiritual to us, we are drawn into activities that allow us to use our gifts to serve others, and we are learning and growing together. We enjoy being together and we are the richer for it. Over and over again I have seen people drawn into the Christian faith by the sheer quality of the community.

This is as it should be. We all need community. We all need

a place "where everybody knows our name." We need an environment that draws us out of ourselves and into responsible, healthy and wholeness-oriented living. The church at its best can be that place.

SIGNIFICANCE

So how do we encounter God in church? The short answer is, by participating in all the activities that characterize a church, with eyes open, listening, noticing, expectant. In this place dedicated to God, with these people who are seeking to follow God, the atmosphere is rich with the Divine.

This question also has a more nuanced answer. Open yourself to all the elements of worship. Rest in the music. Listen carefully to the reading of Scripture and the sermon that seeks to make it plain. Pray. Participate in Holy Communion. In addition, you will want to explore the truth of Christianity. With open mind take advantage of the teaching/learning opportunities available. Participate in the life of the church. Get involved in the outreach ministries. Practice spiritual disciplines, especially those that seem to resonate with you. Go on retreat. Engage in the spiritual practices that characterize those who follow Jesus. Enjoy the fellowship. After all, it is the quality of the community that resounds with Presence. Belong even as you grow in your belief.

Of course all this presupposes that you have found the kind of Christian community that is alive with God. Not all are. Some places only have left a faint echo of what once was life. So search until you find the place that resonates with you in the midst of your spiritual journey.

Conclusion

How Do We Know It Is God?

Okay, was that the voice of God or the voice of your (long dead) mother telling you to do this thing? Would *not* doing it be missing an invitation to a fuller, richer life? Or is this just your imagination gone awry (and so doing it would take you down the wrong path)? To do this thing—would that be a response to God or an act of superstition?

Here is the dilemma once you posit that God can and does communicate with us. *How do you know it is God?* Unfortunately we have a long history of people claiming to hear God's voice and then launching into dumb, crazy or even terrible acts. Remember Jim Jones in Guyana and all those people who drank the poison Kool-Aid, trusting that they were following God? An extreme example, certainly, but it does underwrite the need to know whose voice we are following.

Discernment is what we need: learning to distinguish between the voices, the impulses, the good advice and the intuitions. Discernment is asking, "Is this of God?" Discernment involves putting the pieces of the puzzle together and then _ng with confidence. Discernment means following the path of wisdom not self-deception.

There are really two issues here: discerning God's presence and discerning God's voice. Discerning God's presence is what I mean by noticing God in this world. Learning to live in a God-filled universe brings hope, joy, courage and much else to our life. Discerning God's voice has to do with choices we make: what (if anything) does God have to say about those decisions?

The first challenge involves responding to the God whose presence we discern in the world. How do we reach out to this God whose presence we have experienced? Not responding, consciously and deliberately, can keep our spiritual life in the realm of entertainment rather than transformation. It would be like getting high on God—warm feelings but without impact because there is still a fundamental disconnect between God and us. How do we respond?

The second challenge is discerning God's voice and learning to hear God rightly. It is with this second challenge that I want to begin. In too many tragic situations people claimed to hear God but clearly did not, and the results were disastrous. I want to suggest a series of guidelines that will help us discern if something is "of God" or not.

People Who Claim to Hear God But Obviously Haven't

What about those people who claim that God has told them to do something that is so heinous that we cringe at the very thought? Take the Lafferty brothers, for example—Ron and Dan—who claimed that God told Ron to kill his younger brother Allen's wife, Brenda, along with her baby, Erica. Award-winning writer Jon Krakauer tells their story in great detail in his book *Under the Banner of Heaven: A Story of Violent Faith.*

Here is the revelation that Ron wrote out on a sheet of yellow legal paper:

> Thus Saith the lord unto My servants the Prophets. It is My will and commandment that ye remove the following individuals in order that My work might go forward. For they have truly become obstacles in My path and I will not allow My work to be stopped. First thy brother's wife Brenda and her baby . . .

This was one of approximately twenty revelations that Ron Lafferty received during February and March 1984. Later on Ron received another revelation that he was "the mouth of God" and his brother Dan was the "arm of God." The brothers understood this to mean that Dan would do the actual killing. They also came to understand the reason why Brenda and Erica needed to be killed: they were wicked "children of perdition" who deserved to be killed.[1]

On July 24, 1984, Ron and Dan killed Brenda and Erica. The brothers were apprehended shortly thereafter and charged with murder. Ron and Dan were tried separately. Ron was convicted and sentenced to death. Dan was also convicted but he was given life imprisonment. Dan insisted that he was guilty of no crime although he did not deny killing Brenda and Erica. His claim: "I was doing God's will, which is not a crime."[2]

This is a horrible story, compounded by the fact that the Lafferty brothers calmly blamed their actions on God. To say God has spoken to us is a claim we must make with great care.

I do not want to seem to be pointing a finger at other religious movements—certainly there are few if any Mormons who would be comfortable with the claim by the Lafferty brothers that God commanded them to kill their sister-in-law. Within Christianity there are ample examples of those claiming to hear [illegible]d and who engage in horrendous acts that history later j[illegible] to be misguided. For example, there was Pope Urban II, who in 1095 stirred up the crowds to attack Muslims and thus was born the first crusade with the battle cry of *Deus Vult!* ("God wills it"). Or take John Brown, who heard God call him to battle on behalf of the abolition of slavery. This led to his infamous raid on Harper's Ferry. Right cause, wrong method. Or nearer our own time, there is Paul Hill, who felt God called him to murder an abortion doctor, which he in fact did.[3]

Discernment

Let me reiterate my basic stance when it comes to human and divine interaction. I have come to believe that God communicates to us in many different ways as part of an "intermittent conversation"[4] that unfolds over time. This being the case, discernment involves listening to these various inputs from various sources (the Bible, the still small voice, conversation, logic, music, other people, contemplation, etc.) and then processing with others what we hear and know until we find a sense of clarity. Without active discernment we run the dual risk of attribution (supposing something to be of God when it is not) and narcissism (blaming our desires on God). We need to learn to discern the genuine voice of God. To over-claim is a fearful thing—we are not God; we are not even the mouthpiece of God (except, perhaps, in the very rare and special case of the prophet and even then—especially then—we need humility and doubt). To under-claim, that is, never to notice the abundant presence of God, is also a problem. We cut ourselves off from the wonder, love and transformation that is possible when we are open to God.

So how does discernment work? I wish there was an easy answer to this question. I wish there was a formula I could propose that would enable us to say with certainty, "Now that was God." Alas, we will always continue to be creatures called to walk by faith, and that means never knowing with utter certainty. Still, our faith has to be warranted, not delusional.

I propose three tests that can help us discern whether we are hearing God or not. We need to ask, Is what I am sensing in line with the Word of God, the community of God and the fruit of God?

The Word of God. Christians have long claimed that what we find in the Bible is the revealed truth of God. The Bible is understood to have a special (unique) place in our life and faith. In the Bible we find "true truth." So if the sense we have, if the voice we hear, if the calling we perceive contradicts the clear teaching of Scripture, then Scripture trumps our experience.

Now we have to be careful here. For one thing, we need to be sure we have properly understood what the Bible actually teaches. The Bible has been made to say all sorts of weird and contradictory things, mostly by taking something out of context or by not hearing what is said in the way the original recipients of the message would have understood it. Then there is the problem of letting other people who have an agenda tell us what the Bible supposedly means. Given these cautions, the basis for discernment is the clear teaching of Scripture.

Moreover, many things are clear. For example, I remember a young man saying to me some years ago that if God called him to jump off the Tobin Bridge he would do so without hesitation. Now the Tobin Bridge is a very high bridge in Boston, and to jump from it would certainly result in death. I think that this young man was trying to impress me with how "sold-out to God" he was, in contrast to what he perceived to be my own less-than-committed faith. This one was easy. I said, "Don, if you ever hear God calling you to jump off the Tobin Bridge, you can be sure of one thing—it is not God you are hearing. God has spoken quite

-y already about this matter. God said 'Thou shalt not kill' and this includes not killing yourself." The Ten Commandments are part of the clear teaching of Scripture.

It is not always this easy to discern what Scripture is telling us. Our understanding of the Bible gets confused with wrong assumptions, misunderstood musings, bad teaching, cultural biases and so on. We takes verses out of context and make them mean something they were never meant to mean. We don't always have a good grasp of what the Bible actually means. Therefore, it is important to discuss our understanding of Scripture with others.

The community of God. This leads to my second test: What does our community have to say? Does what you are claiming seem to them to be of God? We need a whole community when it comes to discernment, not just our own unaided opinion.

Interaction with the community takes place on various levels. First, you need to talk to those who know you best. Perhaps this is a small group of which you are a part. In a good small group, over time, people come to know each other. A level of honest sharing and vulnerability develops within a covenant of confidentiality. So when you go to the group and say, "I think God is calling me to become a priest," they can say, "Of course. Why did it take you so long to realize this?" They know you. They love you. They have watched your life unfold. They see your strengths and weaknesses. They know this is the way you are meant to go. Incidentally, I have heard this sort of story from numerous seminary students over the years—how it was close friends in the church who sensed that they had a calling to ministry long before they knew it. Furthermore, it was not uncommon for these very friends who affirmed their call to ministry to go one step further and help support them financially while they were in seminary.

Second, you may need to bring up the issue with the leadership of the community—the men and women who are leaders by dint of training, experience, calling and skill. Often such people have the kind of overview and perspective that brings wise insight to bear on your questions. Certain groups like the Quakers (who take this matter of hearing God very seriously) have processes in place to deal with discernment. The Clearness Committee is one example. A member brings a question to the leadership ("I have been offered two jobs. I am wrestling with the question of which to take," is a not infrequent kind of question in such circumstances.) A committee is appointed. The questioner prepares a document for the committee containing the facts of the matter. The committee convenes and a whole process of listening is undertaken before they come to any conclusion. The early church made such decisions a matter of "prayer and fasting." For example, Paul and Barnabas were sent on a missionary journey when the church at Antioch discerned through worship, prayer and fasting that the Holy Spirit had called them to this work (Acts 13:1-3).

Third, you may want to consult a spiritual director. A spiritual director is a person who has the gift of discernment and has undergone training in this particular form of ministry. There is a long tradition of spiritual direction in the church dating back to the desert fathers and mothers. Certain monastic orders such as the Benedictines and the Jesuits have produced gifted spiritual directors. The goal of spiritual direction is to help the directee discern the voice of God in his or her life.

Of course, we have to be careful when we take our questions of discernment to the community. The problem when it comes to trusting the insights and sensibilities of those in your Christian community is that Christian communities can become self-serving and blind to themselves. When all are of the same mindset, the discernment they bring to an issue may reflect their own biases and wishes. They are not disinterested discerners, and so their input must be taken cautiously.

The fruit of God. The third test has to do with fruit: "You will know them by their fruits" (Matthew 7:16-20). Jesus makes this statement in the Sermon on the Mount. He is talking here about false prophets who would lead people astray, pretending to speak in God's name. Jesus says that such people come "in sheep's clothing but inwardly are ravenous wolves." What a great image: fierce wolves intent on devouring us, dressed as gentle, harmless sheep! We certainly require discernment lest we be led into danger. By means of colorful language Jesus points out why it is so important to know God's voice over against other voices. Those other voices could be intent on doing us harm.

Jesus then goes on to say that good trees bear good fruit while bad trees bear bad fruit. This is the question we must ask ourselves. What will be the outcome should you act upon what you think God is saying to you? Will it produce good fruit or bad fruit? Will the outcome be good for you and for others? If so, chances are this is from God.

However, with this third test, we must beware of unintended consequences. We can be deceived at this point too, as well as with the first two tests. Anticipating good fruit when any disinterested observer would see that only bad fruit will come gets us into trouble. Being willfully blind because you want to do something despite its consequences is dangerous.

So, boiled down to its essence, discernment involves asking three questions: what does the Bible say, what does my community say, and will there be good outcomes if I go this way? In addition we need to be aware that none of these tests is infallible!

Ignatian Discernment

St. Ignatius has a lot to say about discernment. Remember him from the second chapter—the founder of the Jesuits? The Jesuit movement has a rich tradition of spiritual direction, arising out of the *Spiritual Exercises*, where Ignatius offers rules for discernment.

In the *Spiritual Exercises*, Ignatius talks about what he calls "the three states of the soul" that enable us to make good decisions when faced with a choice.[5] When we are in one of these three states, he says, we are able to discern God's will.

In the first state, when God speaks clearly to us (as in a mystical experience), the path is clear and self-evident. Ignatius uses the conversion of St. Paul as the example of what he means here. Paul's mystical encounter with the risen Christ left no doubt in Paul's mind that he was to follow Jesus and that he was called to take the gospel message to the Gentiles. No ambiguity here. Second, we know what to do when we have been given sufficient light via "consolation and desolation." Consolation and desolation are Ignatian terms for the affect that comes to us in prayer by which, under the guidance of a spiritual director, the mind of Christ is made clear to us.[6] We come to know via our inward disposition what God would have us do. The third state of the soul within which we make godly decisions comes when we are at peace with ourselves and in a state of "indifference." By "indifference" Ignatius means that we have reached the place that we have no inclination one way or another. Our desire is to be one with God's desire.

In this state of indifference (the third state) Ignatius then proposes five rules we can use to discern what choice to make. First, we need to be clear that our only motivation is the love of God. Second, in our imagination we ask ourselves how we would advise someone who came to us asking about this choice.

Third, still in our imagination, we are to think about how we would feel about this choice when we are at the point of death. Fourth, we imagine another scenario: how would we feel about each side of the choice at the Last Judgment? Finally, when all this is clear, we simply choose to the best of our ability.

But how do we know we are right? Ignatius tells us that we must just trust. We must have faith that we have made the right decision. We might receive positive confirmation from God, but then again we might not. No matter, just trust. "If God does not indicate to me interiorly that my choice is contrary to his will, I shall consider it conformed to his will."[7] In other words, don't sweat it. Get on with life. If the decision is wrong, that is God's issue. You have done all you could to the best of your ability.

I find this advice very sensible. In the end, it comes down to trust. In those instances when I have tried to follow Ignatius's guidance on making a choice, it has worked out well.

Methodist Discernment

The Methodist Quadrilateral is a method of discernment credited to John Wesley, the eighteenth-century founder of the Methodist Church (although the term itself comes from the Methodist scholar Albert Outler). Outler says that Wesley used four sources to discern theological truth: the Bible, tradition, reason and experience. As the *Methodist Book of Discipline* puts it, "Wesley believed that the living core of the Christian faith was revealed in Scripture, illumined by tradition, vivified in personal experience, and confirmed by reason. Scripture [however] is primary, revealing the Word of God so far as it is necessary for our salvation."[8]

Again, one begins with the Bible. We ask, What does Scripture have to say about this matter? We then move to the two-thousand-year tradition of the church. What have others said when facing the same thing? Third, we think about it. Does this make sense? We use our God-given mind. Finally, what does experience teach us? Does all this fit with what we know of God?

Discernment is crucial in order to avoid misguided behavior which we then attribute to God. However, there is no such thing as absolute certainty. We try our best to verify that this is "of God," and then we walk by faith into the future, trusting that God is leading us.

Of course, different situations require different levels of discernment. On the really big issues—call, relocation, marriage, tragic moral choices (when neither option is the best), lifestyle alteration—we need to devote significant time, energy and process to hearing God as clearly as we can. On the other end of the spectrum, Scripture and tradition have already made a great deal very clear concerning moral behavior, relationships, speech and so forth. We just have to get on with the doing of it. We hesitate because we may not want to do what we know we should do. But most of the time discernment is just a matter of listening carefully, over time, so that we develop a pretty good sense of what God is doing in our lives. Community is essential to us. Others will help us chart a wise course if we let them be part of the process.

Responding to God

The second question involves responding to God's presence in the world. Noticing God is one thing, responding is another. What is it that drives us to move from observer to follower? What motivates us to reach out to the God we encounter?

According to Barbara Bradley Hagerty, one answer is *brokenness*. Brokenness is the tipping point for many people. In the course of numerous interviews, Hagerty found this to be the most common antecedent to spiritual transformation.

> ness occurs when life—in the form of addiction, cer, singleness, unemployment, or indefinable misery—defeats you. It happens when you come to the end of yourself, you have exhausted your own resources, your own strength and resilience to cope with the situation at hand. You surrender and in that place of release, you find a strange calm. It is the only way that many a stubborn soul finds God.[9]

Longing also opens us up to God—longing for "more" in life, longing for purpose and meaning, longing to matter. Of course, we can achieve satisfaction in all sorts of ways—through loving relationships, enjoyable experiences and fulfilling work—and all this is good. But over time we encounter a deeper longing: a longing to be connected to the root of our being. As Gerald May describes this: "For all of us . . . there are moments of dawning awareness, little cracks in our armor that reveal glimpses of our deeper longings. . . . Maybe we've been grasping for good things, when what we've really desired is the Creator of all good things."[10] In God we discover our gifts, we discern our destiny, and we find our place in the world.

Wonder also draws us to God. Wonder at the universe in which we live, wonder at the God-encounters we experience, wonder at the world of the Spirit that is opening up before us. It is like we are starting to see in a new way. Our eyes are being opened. In noticing the radiance we once were blind to, we reach out of ourselves with a desire to be a part of this new world, this world of the Spirit.

How, then, do we respond to God? God is not just a presence to discern but a being to encounter. God is not just a powerful force to be accessed (from whom we gain energy and emotion), but rather a person who invites us into relationship (communion, union). How do we enter into the way of transformation?

Curiously, many of the people in the Greeley/McCready study on mystical experiences (mentioned in chapter one) failed to respond to the God they met in those mystical moments. It was as if the experience itself was enough. On one level, this is true. By virtue of that encounter they revised their view of death. Death no longer held the same terror it once did. But what if they had said *yes* to this God they met in the mystical moment? What if they sought to develop a relationship with God? Encountering God is one thing; responding to God is another.

Different people are at different places with the God-question. If in your noticing you find yourself searching to know God, many avenues lie open to you. Follow the way that resonates with you. If it is, for example, the argument of design (in the universe) that excites you, explore these intellectual arguments. If it is sitting on a beach in California when the sun goes down, use that beauty to open the way to God. If it is the buzz of involvement with others in the midst of a community of worship and service that gives you a sense of meaning, let the community open the way of God for you. There are lots of avenues. The challenge is to explore, to engage with the issue, to press on. Inertia is the enemy of spiritual transformation—allowing ourselves to be distracted by the "things of this world," so we never get on with the search for the other world.

If all else fails, why not pray? "God, reveal yourself to me." See what happens. The Bible says, "Draw near to God, and [God] will draw near to you" (James 4:8).

God Revealed

Where are we now in this journey of noticing God? We have seen God revealed in the following avenues:

- God is revealed via dramatic encounters we call mystical experiences (but these are the exception, not the rule).
- God is also revealed in the midst of the texture of our daily life, filled as it is with hints, intuitions, gifts of grace, love and the other signs of Presence.
- As we learn to notice God in the midst of daily life, so too we become alert to the still small voice within us—the whispers of God.
- In community with others, these whispers find shape and meaning as we seek together to live as God's people (which all of us are by dint of having been made in the image of God). We touch the presence of God by means of the actualized love of others. This love takes concrete form in spiritual fruits such as love, joy, peace and long-suffering and by means of spiritual gifts such as hospitality, wisdom and healing.
- In community we open ourselves to the Bible, which is alive with the presence of God.
- So too we see God in nature in various manifestations: the wonder of the created world; the unfolding of human culture with its curious fascination with God; the power of creativity, which itself flows from God; and the struggle to grasp real reality and give this vision shape via painting, music, dance, poetry and other artistic expressions.
- God is certainly manifest in the various aspects of the church of Jesus Christ—worship, teaching, fellowship, retreat and service—as we gather to live together as people seeking God.

What does all this add up to? God is an elusive presence. Hints, encounters, intuitions—God is so tantalizingly close at times, yet just when we seem to grasp God, God disappears (or so it seems). Why? Why not stay present? Why not touch our lives with that constant aura of otherness that brings such rich vitality to life? Why isn't the supernatural world as vivid and present as this world of sight, sound and touch? Why is it that when we encounter for a moment the raw Otherness where we know we belong, it vanishes when we look away just for a moment?

All this has to do with *faith* I suppose, with the fact that we were created to be people of faith. "Walk by faith, not by sight." Sight is a strange thing. Adam and Eve lived within sight of God and that did not work out so well. The Genesis story seems to say that living within the immediate presence of God is a great challenge for us as human beings. My friend David R. Nelson puts it this way:

> Maybe it has something to do with growing up. If God made us in his image and gave us the freedom to make choices then we need to be able to make choices. If God were not elusive would we make choices or would we even recognize that we were making choices? Would we ever become responsible human beings with whom God might enjoy a conversation? I remember Harry Strachan saying that it was very hard to have a rational conversation about a set of blueprints when faced with "I think God wants us to put the door there." C. S. Lewis had it right. You can't walk around in heaven until your feet are solid enough not to get cut by the grass.[11]

Perhaps this lack of immediate access to the world of the supernatural has to do with learning to be present in this wonderful empirical world that God created for us. It is not just that we find it hard to live in two worlds; we also find it hard to live fully in this present world. We drift. We float. We seek vivid experiences to connect us to this world because it so easy just to walk through life without noticing much. We need to learn to notice this world just as surely as we need to learn to notice that other world. Two worlds. Perhaps God wants us to learn to live first in this world, as a way of preparing us to live fully in that other world.

The classical view of the spiritual journey points in this direction. It begins with *purgation:* learning to live fully in a world filled with temptation and trial. Then it moves to *illumination,* during which we engage in those acts of love and service that reveal the power and reality of that other world. Only when we (or when the few) move into what is called *union* do we begin to merge into the world of the Spirit. Those considered to be great saints at times seem loosely connected to this world, as if they are listening to haunting music that we can only faintly discern. Those who have journeyed that far have much to teach us. We too need to learn to listen, to discern the melodies of that other sphere of reality within which our lives are bathed. Those tones, which I think are clear and present when we are small children, grow more remote and distant as the tunes of this present age grow in volume in our lives. We need to learn to listen again to the deeper music of existence.

Perhaps this lack of continuous presence has to do with learning to love more deeply. The Great Commandment is quite clear: love God, love others and love self. Perhaps we need to notice God in others as a way of growing in love. Clearly we need to love others if we say we love God. Loving others is the sign that we love God (John 15:12-17).

This was one of the great lessons Mother Teresa has taught us. As a young woman she had a clear sense of God's presence, which included mystical visions of various sorts. But later in life, after she had established the Missionaries of Charity (in response to the leading of God), she lost that sense of presence.

There was a "terrible darkness within," she reports, one that brought her great anguish.[12] Her response, however, was not to withdraw from her work.

> Instead of stifling her missionary impulse, the darkness seemed to invigorate it. Mother Teresa understood the anguish of the human soul that felt the absence of God, and she yearned to light the light of Christ's love in the "dark hole" of every heart buried in desperation, loneliness, or rejection. She recognized that whatever her interior state, God's tender care was always there, manifested through the small favors others did for her or unexpected conveniences that accompanied her undertakings.[13]

She loved God whom she no longer experienced by loving those she had been sent to love—the poor and the dying.

We walk by faith not by sight. Yet those times of "sight" are a great gift to be cherished but held loosely. One day, when we go through the gate of death, it will be "all sight." But for the present, we are being prepared for that day.

The Spiritual Gift of Noticing God

So we are called to engage in the process of noticing God. As I have said, I consider this a spiritual discipline. The spiritual discipline of noticing God is the discipline that underlies all the other disciplines. Is this not what we seek each week in common worship together—to know and experience God? Is this not what we seek in Bible reading and prayer—communion with the living God? Is not this our calling then—to engage in the spiritual discipline of noticing God?

Out of such noticing flows transformation. As we touch the reality of God, in small and large ways, that reality transforms us. And thus we seek that Presence that changes us. We know that God is for us and present to us, even as we know that God's presence is not always easily accessible—sometimes for reasons within us, sometimes for reasons within the will of God. But for our part, we are called to keep on keeping on. To be present to God and to this world and to each other and to that other world—this is our calling, as we seek to become whole.

God wants us to be whole.

Acknowledgments

Special thanks goes to those whose input helped me make this a better book.

First of all I want to thank my wife, Judy Boppell Peace, an author in her own right, for all the conversations we had about noticing God. Her questions often sent me searching for more insight. She was my first reader. Her editing made each chapter more precise. Judy also came up with the book's title.

Special thanks also goes to my longtime friend and colleague David R. Nelson. He patiently worked his way through each chapter. He rewrote sentences and sections as well as helping me correct structural problems in several chapters, especially chapter six, "Creation, Culture and Creativity."

I also owe special thanks to my colleagues at Fuller Theological Seminary Dr. Robert Johnston and Dr. William Dyrness for reading chapter six and offering many valuable comments. Their perspective on natural revelation can be found in the new book by William Dyrness, *Poetic Theology: God and the Poetics of Everyday Life* (Eerdmans, 2011) and in the forthcoming and yet to be named volume on natural revelation by Rob Johnston.

Special thanks also to my daughter Dr. Jennifer Howe Peace and my son-in-law Dr. Joe Tito whose insightful reading strengthened the final draft. I also want to thank Dr. David Robinson for sharing his expertise on Benedictine spirituality, which was a great aid in writing chapter four. And thanks as well to InterVarsity Press and the thoughtful attention they have given to this book (and to all my books that they have published), especially Cindy Bunch with her keen editorial sense, Cindy Kiple for her fine design work and Susan Wood for her careful copyediting.

Finally there are all the students at Fuller Theological Seminary and Gordon-Conwell Theological Seminary with whom I have talked about these matters over the years in various courses I taught on spirituality. Their comments, questions and sharing of their own stories of God-encounters helped me sharpen and broaden my own thinking. I also want to thank the men's group at Wenham Congregational Church in Wenham, Massachusetts, who allowed me to lead a retreat based on the book and then gave me valuable feedback.

Pentecost, 2011

A Guide for Personal Reflection and Group Discussion

The Spiritual Discipline of Noticing God

What follows is a series of questions related to each of the chapters. These questions have two uses. First, they can serve as a guide to personal reflection. It is one thing to read a chapter; it is another to connect that chapter to one's own life. I hope that this book will aid readers to engage in the spiritual discipline of noticing God. We need all the help we can get when it comes to ascertaining the presence of God (at least I do). I see these questions as a kind of help.

Second, the questions can be used in the context of a small group. Intentional small groups are a powerful format in which to seek to discern God. Certainly this has been my experience. Small groups, when properly run, generate the kind of conversation we all long for. This being the case, I will begin by describing how to structure a small group that works.

Creating a Small Group

Good small groups are organized around a topic of deep interest to all the members. So if you are setting up a small group, be sure to describe clearly the nature of this group when you invite people to join. For example: "We are going to meet together to discuss the topic of noticing God. We will be using a book by that title to stimulate our own conversation. Each week we will all read a chapter and then come together to talk about what we read. This is a kind of book group. If this interests you, we'd love to have you join us."

Good small groups work at fostering community. The aim of the small group should be not only to study *Noticing God,* but also to share personal stories that relate to the theme of each chapter. These stories will bring to life the ideas in the chapter. Community building comes by hearing each other's stories.

Good small groups are the right size. By definition a small group consists of between five and thirteen people, seated in such a way that each person can see the eyes of the others. Under five members, the group does not have enough diversity of ideas and experience for a really effective group conversation; over thirteen, not enough time is available for all to speak fully.

Good small groups eat together. Begin the first meeting with a potluck dinner. Eating together creates community and helps a group of strangers quickly become a group of friends. In fact, each week you should share food together. This can be as modest as cold drinks and store-bought cookies or as elaborate as a sit-down dinner. Structure this in whatever way works best for your group.

Good small groups foster focused discussion by using carefully chosen questions. Use the questions that follow to guide your discussion. There are two general types of question: those that focus on the book and what it is saying (and thus generate the idea-oriented discussion); and those that focus on application (and help group members make connections to their own lives). It is important to keep the conversation focused. Otherwise the group becomes a kind of social gathering. There is nothing wrong with that, but unguided discussion seldom yields the quality of conversation that is possible when a group of interested (and interesting) people talk through important issues.

Good small groups have a leader who knows how to draw everyone into the discussion. The small group leader is not the teacher; he or she is the conversation facilitator. There are four challenges when it comes to guiding a good group conversation:

1. *Getting started:* Here is where the opening, relational questions come into play. Go around the circle, beginning with the leader, and let each person respond briefly to the opening question. These questions are designed to help people share brief stories related to the topic at hand. In this way everyone gets to talk.

2. *Keeping focused:* It is easy to meander. The job of the leader is to keep drawing the group back to the issues at hand by the judicious use of questions.

3. *Engaging everyone:* The aim is a group conversation in which each person participates. Sometimes the problem is that a few of the over-talkative folk (whose energy helpfully fuels the conversation) may take over the conversation. The group leader needs to rein them in. The other problem has to do with the shy people, who need encouragement to join in the conversation.

4. *Sticking to the schedule:* Start on time, end on time, and make sure the important issues get discussed. The group leader is the tour guide who keeps the conversation moving on track and on time. (Of course, sometimes the discussion gets to be so deep that the group will agree to extra time for the sake of the process.)

Using the Questions

Each small group session, as described below, has three parts: opening sharing, analysis of a chapter in *Noticing God* and reflection on the meaning of the chapter. Each aspect requires a different sort of question.

Opening questions. Good small groups, as I already mentioned, begin with brief personal sharing. Such sharing builds community, gives each person a voice and gets the group focused on the topic

Analysis questions. Good small groups focus on topics of worth. The second part of the small group discussion revolves around a particular chapter in the book. The questions are designed to make sure everyone understands what has been said and what it all means. This discussion explores the material in the book. Of course it goes without saying that the more carefully each group member has read the chapter, the better the conversation will be.

Reflection questions. Good small groups move from ideas to application: what does all this mean to each person? Here is where stories get told, questions get discussed and new options present themselves. This is the "so what?" part of the conversation—linking the ideas of the chapter to the life of the group members. In the end, the goal of the discussion is not just deeper understanding (which is important) but deeper openness to the God who meets us where we are.

STRUCTURING THE SMALL GROUP

Choosing questions. There are more questions for each chapter than any one group can use. The aim is not to answer all these questions (so as to complete a "task"), but rather to use selected questions to drive a conversation. So the group leader will want to think about the most important questions to ask in terms of his or her particular group.

Some questions have several parts to them. At times you will want to ask each part of the question separately. At other times you will want to ask the question in its totality. Asking questions is the role of the leader, but this is no big deal since everyone has a copy of *Noticing God* and can read the questions on their own.

Generic questions. The more focused the question, the better the discussion. But there are certain questions that can be asked in almost any discussion:

- In what ways do the ideas in this chapter connect with you?
- What questions did this chapter raise for you?
- Have you had an experience similar to those described in this chapter? If so, share it briefly with the group.
- What is your personal response to the assertions in this chapter?
- What is the next step for you in light of these ideas?
- How do you respond to what was just said? (Such a question can draw shy people into the conversation.)

Time schedule. What follows is material for nine small group sessions. If nine weeks are not available you might consider combining various sessions. Or you can skip certain chapters, asking participants to read the missing chapters and work through the questions on their own.

Small groups seem to work best that meet weekly.

Each small group session is designed to last between 45 and 90 minutes. Here is how to structure the discussion with various time formats:

- *90-minute small group:* Opening (15 minutes), Analysis (30 minutes), Reflection (45 minutes)
- *60-minute small group:* Opening (15 minutes), Analysis (20 minutes), Reflection (25 minutes)
- *45-minute small group:* Opening (10 minutes), Analysis (15 minutes), Reflection (20 minutes)

The Questions

Introduction

HOW DO WE NOTICE THE PRESENCE OF GOD?

Opening

1. Introduce yourself to the group by quickly giving basic facts about yourself: what you do, where you live, who you live with and how you came to be in this group.
2. Why did you join this group, and what do you want from it?

Analysis

3. What do you make of this whole idea of "the habitual presence of God"? Does this excite you? Distress you? Challenge you? Explain.
4. What is the "spiritual discipline of noticing God" all about?
5. Which of the seven chapters described in the introduction interests you the most and why?
6. Which of the core assumptions resonates most deeply with you and why? Which challenges you the most? Which surprises you?

Reflection

7. In the introduction I describe my fascination with the idea of God-encounters that led to writing this book. How would you account for your own interest in this topic?

8. Read aloud the quotation from Thomas Merton with which the introduction begins. How do you respond to what Merton has to say?

Chapter 1
MYSTICAL ENCOUNTERS

Opening

1. Which word(s) best describes where you are when it comes to the question of God? Explain your answer.

❑ Convinced	❑ Searching	❑ Open
❑ Unconvinced	❑ Troubled	❑ Hopeful
❑ Perplexed	❑ Angry	❑ Wondering
❑ Longing	❑ Unfulfilled	❑ Other ________

2. Where are you now in your spiritual quest?

Analysis

3. This chapter told various stories about people who had mystical experiences. If possible, share other such stories of mystical experiences by people you know or have read about. Then describe what you make of these accounts. (Sharing your own experiences comes later in the discussion.)
4. Three general types of mystical experiences are described: dramatic encounters, brushes with the Divine and stabs of longing for the Other. Discuss the difference between each type of experience.
5. What do you make of the research on the role of the brain when it comes to spiritual experiences?

6. What is the value of mystical experiences?

Reflection

7. Have you ever had a mystical experience of one sort or another? If you feel comfortable sharing this, describe what happened and what it meant to you. If you have not had anything like a mystical experience, how do you respond to such stories?
8. Sir Alister Hardy asked people to send him personal accounts of experiences in which they were influenced "by some Power, whether they call it God or not, which may either appear to be beyond their individual selves or partly, or even entirely, within their being." What might you have written to him (if anything)?
9. William James says that a mystical experience has four qualities: it is ineffable (hard to describe), noetic (brings profound insight), transient (it does not last long) and passive (it comes upon one). How well do each of these traits describe your own experience (or that of others you know about)?
10. Is the "world alive with God" for you? If so, how? If not, what do you make of this concept?

Chapter 2
GOD IN THE ORDINARY

Opening

1. What do you know about Jesus, and how did you come to

know this? Has your encounter with Jesus been good, bad or neutral? Why?

Analysis

2. What does the Jesuit mantra of "finding God in all things" mean to you? Is this realistic? Possible? Desirable?
3. This chapter asserts that spiritual formation is, in part, about becoming more and more conscious. Do you agree or disagree? How does one become more conscious? How does the prayer of examen aid in such a task?
4. What is the role of imagination in the process of spiritual formation? In what ways (if any) have you used your imaginative faculty to grow spiritually? Discuss the power of imagination.
5. How do you understand the assertion that in meeting Jesus we meet God in human form?

Reflection

6. This chapter is about meeting Jesus. Where are you, personally, when it comes to Jesus? What do you feel about Jesus and why?
7. How do you understand this whole idea of encountering God in everyday life? How do you experience this reality?

Prayer Exercises: A Personal Challenge

It is one thing to read about Ignatian prayer exercises that open us up to spiritual reality. It is another to experience these various forms of prayer. So why not try out one or more of these exercises before the next small group discussion? See what happens. In the next small group meeting you will get a chance to share what you experienced (if you choose to do so).

1. ***Prayer of examen.*** Take 15 minutes or so and follow the step-by-step process outlined in this chapter for the prayer of examen. At first it may feel awkward, but with just a little practice it becomes easy and natural. Do not neglect the journaling aspect of the exercise.

2. ***Ignatian contemplation.*** Follow the process outlined in this chapter. See what fruits your imagination can bring forth as you imagine meeting Jesus in the context of one of the Gospel stories. Begin with the baptism of Jesus as discussed in this chapter.

3. ***Spiritual direction.*** Not everyone is called to have a spiritual director, but if this idea attracts you at all, explore the possibility of linking up with a spiritual director. Check out Spiritual Directors International at www.sdiworld.org/ for help in locating a spiritual director.

4. ***Spiritual exercises.*** Look for a Jesuit retreat center in your area. There one can participate in a retreat based on the *Spiritual Exercises*. You do not need to be limited to Jesuit centers though. A personal retreat at almost any retreat center has the potential to bring good fruit.

5. ***Relationship with Jesus.*** In your journal, take time to describe your relationship with Jesus or your desire for a relationship with Jesus or your perplexity about this whole idea of a relationship with Jesus.

- How do you feel about Jesus? Why?
- What do you know about Jesus? What do you want to know about Jesus?
- What is Jesus calling you to do or be now?

Chapter 3
THE STILL SMALL VOICE

Opening

1. Where are you at this point in time with regard to the idea of God interacting with us as human beings? Share your reflections.
2. If you tried out any of the Ignatian prayer exercises during the previous week, share your experience. If you did not try out any of these exercises, discuss that as well.

Analysis

3. Read aloud 1 Kings 19. Then discuss verses 11-13 (which are found in chapter three). How do you understand the nature of the "still small voice" described here? What is this? Sum up what you know and believe.
4. One of the issues raised here concerns the relationship between the hints and intuitions that all people seem to have (though some are more adept at noticing these than others) and the still small voice of God.
   - Can you identify in your own experience examples of intuitions that have served you well?
   - Have you had experiences of what you took to be the still small voice of God? How did these differ from other experiences?

Reflection

5. In this chapter I have told a number of stories, my own and those of others. What are your stories? Do you have a story that parallels any of these stories?
   - The experience of writing a book (or another artistic creation)

- Hearing a still small voice
- Having a precognitive dream
- Receiving a "message from God" from another person
- Hearing God speak via a dream
- A divine compulsion or conviction
- Receiving from God a message as specific as an outline of a book

Share your story with the group. What impact did this experience have on you?

6. Something as subjective as hearing the still small voice of God is bound to raise questions. How do you respond to some of the questions I have asked in the chapter? What other questions do you have?
   - How do we distinguish God's voice from other inner voices?
   - How do we know when an inner voice is God?
   - How do we distinguish ordinary convictions from divine convictions?
   - What are the dangers of asserting that God told you something?

Chapter 4
THE POWER OF COMMUNITY

Opening

Our lives are filled with people. If we indeed meet God in

others, as I believe to be the case, then we need to reflect on the texture and character of our relational world.

1. Who in your life has truly loved you? How was that love expressed? How were you shaped by that love?
2. Of people you have met, about whom would you say, "Christ is in that person"? or "God is alive in that person"? What qualities in that person led you to this conclusion?

Analysis

3. This chapter focuses on Benedictine spirituality. Share your experience with Benedictines or other monastics (if any). Discuss monasticism. Does this way of life appeal to you? Seem unrealistic to you? In what ways might the practice of "mindfulness" (encountering God via fixed-hour prayer, *lectio divina*, etc.) enable you to notice God?
4. Discuss the Benedictine assertion that we meet Christ in others. What does this mean? How does this happen?

Reflection

5. Of the nine spiritual fruits Paul names (love, joy, peace, patience, kindness, goodness, faithfulness, gentleness and self-control), which is your strength? Which is your weakness? How might these spiritual fruits manifest the presence of Christ to others?
6. As you think about spiritual gifts, recall those moments in which your skill or ability seemed to transcend your own natural abilities. How is Christ present in your use of spiritual gifts?
7. Who are the crucial people in your world of relationships? In what ways can you inhabit this world, seeking to see Christ in others as well as to serve others in the name of Christ?

Chapter 5
THE WRITTEN WORD

Opening

1. What is your own history when it comes to the Bible? Reflect on your contact (or lack of contact) with the Bible. How has the Bible helped (or hindered) your own search for God? What role does the Bible play in your life at this point in time?

Analysis

2. In the Gospel accounts we hear the voice of Jesus. What is it about the teaching of Jesus, the life of Jesus or the nature of Jesus that makes the most sense to you? How does the Jesus of the New Testament differ from the Jesus of popular culture?
3. If asked to describe the nature of God based on what is found in the Bible, what would you say?
4. What are the characteristics of God-encounters as described in the Bible?

Reflection

5. Have you encountered God or Jesus in some way when reading or hearing the Bible? If so, describe your experience. If not, what is your take on God-encounters via the Bible?
6. "The Bible is the primary means by which we encounter the voice of God." What do you make of this assertion? What is the challenge for you regarding the Bible?

Bible Study: A Personal Exploration

During the week between small group discussions, try your hand at delving into the Bible via focused study and active reflection (as recommended in chapter five).

1. Read the Gospel of Mark in one sitting. Then spend some time writing in your journal seeking to answer the question, Who, then, is Jesus?
2. Explore some of the passages in the Bible that describe God-encounters. Really study these passages so as to grasp their meaning. What do these passages say to you about your own search for God?
3. Engage in focused study and active reflection on the Bible. Choose a passage from Mark, one of the stories that resonated with you when you read the Gospel, and study it in this way.

Chapter 6
CREATION, CULTURE AND CREATIVITY

Opening

1. Laird Hamilton and Susan Casey describe their experience with big waves in almost religious terms. Share an awe-inspiring experience you have had with the majesty, power, beauty or grandeur of nature.
2. If you engaged in Bible study and reflection this past week, share the fruits of that exploration with the group.

Analysis

3. In what ways does creation give us hints about the nature of God?
4. How do cultural products such as art, film, music and liter-

ature give witness to the nature and character of God?

5. Identify particular films, TV shows, music, art, architecture, poetry, fiction and so on that raise the God-question or reveal transcendence.

Reflection

6. Some people are better than others at discerning the presence of God within creation. How sensitive are you to nature? What hints of God's presence have you experienced in nature?
7. Pick one of the following questions to respond to:
   - Are you an artist? Have you found God via the path of creativity? Describe your experience.
   - What about film, music, art, dance and so forth? Where do you find spiritual meaning in the world of pop culture or high culture? Where have you sensed God lurking in art, film, music or literature?
   - Have you followed the path of reason (intellect, cognition) in order to seek to know about God? Describe your experience.
   - What does your conscience tell you about God?

Chapter 7
Church

Opening

1. Identify the Christian groups in which you participated over time, if any. Did such participation bring life and meaning to

you? Or pain, confusion and exclusion? Where are you now when it comes to the church?

Analysis

2. Why is it that the church has such a mixed reputation today? Why do we need an organized form of Christianity?
3. In what ways is God revealed in the context of worship?
4. In what ways do sacraments such as baptism, marriage, funerals and Communion (Eucharist) reveal God?

Reflection

5. In those worship services you have attended, what resonates most with you personally: music, sermon, Scripture, prayer, Communion? How? Why?
6. How have you explored the truth claims of Christianity (in church or in other contexts)? What makes sense? What questions do you have? How can you take the next step in your inquiry?
7. What spiritual disciplines and/or spiritual practices have you engaged in, if any? With what outcomes? What works for you?
8. What has been your experience with Christian fellowship?

Conclusion
HOW DO WE KNOW IT IS GOD?

Opening

1. What has this small group meant to you? What is your best

or most meaningful memory of the time you have spent together?

Analysis

2. What is discernment and why do we need it?
3. Discuss each of the three tests of discernment and how each helps us know whether what we are sensing is "of God" or not.
4. What is Ignatian discernment and how does it work? What is Methodist discernment and how does it work?

Reflection

5. Can you share an experience from your life in which discernment was needed or sought?
6. In your own life, has brokenness, longing, wonder or something else led you to seek God? Illustrate what you mean.
7. Of the seven avenues for noticing God described in this book, which has been most fruitful for you? Why?
8. In summary, where are you now on the question of noticing God? What is the next step for you in your spiritual journey?

It would be good to end your small group by celebrating together in a way that is appropriate for your group.

Further Reading

Here are some key books that offer more depth on the theme of each chapter.

Introduction: How Do We Notice the Presence of God?

Hagerty, Barbara Bradley. *Fingerprints of God: The Search for the Science of Spirituality*. New York: Riverhead Books/Penguin, 2009.

Johnson, Elizabeth. *Quest for the Living God: Mapping Frontiers in the Theology of God*. New York: Continuum, 2008.

Chapter 1: Mystical Encounters

Greeley, Andrew M. *Ecstasy: A Way of Knowing*. Englewood Cliffs, N.J.: Prentice-Hall, 1974.

James, William. *The Varieties of Religious Experience*. 1902. Various editions.

Kerr, Hugh T., and John Mulder, eds. *Famous Conversions*. Grand Rapids: Eerdmans, 1983.

Lewis, C. S. *Mere Christianity*. San Francisco: HarperSanFrancisco, 2001.

Peace, Richard. *Conversion in the New Testament: Paul and the Twelve*. Grand Rapids: Eerdmans, 1999.

Chapter 2: God in the Ordinary

Lowney, Chris. *Heroic Leadership: Best Practices from a 450-Year-Old*

Company that Changed the World. Chicago: Loyola Press, 2003.
Martin, James. *The Jesuit Guide to (Almost) Everything: Spirituality for Real Life*. San Francisco: HarperOne, 2010.
Thibodeaux, Mark E., S.J. *Armchair Mystic: Easing into Contemplative Prayer*. Cincinnati: St. Anthony Messenger Press, 2001.
Warner, Larry. *Journey with Jesus: Discovering the Spiritual Exercises of Saint Ignatius*. Downers Grove, Ill.: InterVarsity Press, 2010.

Chapter 3: The Still Small Voice

Hybels, Bill. *The Power of a Whisper: Hearing God, Having the Guts to Respond*. Grand Rapids: Zondervan, 2010.
Johnson, Ben Campbell. *Living Before God: Deepening Our Sense of the Divine Presence*. Grand Rapids: Eerdmans, 2000.
Lindskoog, Kathryn Ann. *The Gift of Dreams*. San Francisco: HarperCollins, 1979.
Smith, Gordon. *The Voice of Jesus: Discernment, Prayer and the Witness of the Spirit*. Downers Grove, Ill.: InterVarsity Press, 2003.
Tucker, Ruth A. *God Talk: Caution for Those Who Hear God's Voice*. Downers Grove, Ill.: InterVarsity Press, 2005.
Willard, Dallas. *In Search of Guidance: Developing a Conversational Relationship with God*. San Francisco: HarperSanFrancisco, 1993. This book was later reissued as *Hearing God*.

Chapter 4: The Power of Community

de Waal, Esther. *Seeking God: The Way of St. Benedict*. Collegeville, Minn.: Liturgical Press, 1984.
Robinson, David. *Ancient Paths: Discover Christian Formation the Benedictine Way*. Brewster, Mass.: Paraclete Press, 2010.
———. *The Busy Family's Guide to Spirituality: Practical Lessons for Modern Living from the Monastic Tradition*. New York: Crossroad, 2009.
Stewart, Columba. *Prayer and Community: The Benedictine Tradition*. Maryknoll, N.Y.: Orbis, 1998.
Tickle, Phyllis. *The Divine Hours* (in three volumes: *Prayers for Summertime, Prayers for Springtime* and *Prayers for Autumn and Wintertime)*. New York: Doubleday, 2000.

Chapter 5: The Written Word

Bockmuehl, Klaus. *Listening to the God Who Speaks*. Colorado Springs: Helmers & Howard, 1990.

Mulholland, M. Robert. *Shaped by the Word: The Power of Scripture in Spiritual Formation*. Nashville: Upper Room Books, 1986.

Peace, Richard. *Contemplative Bible Reading: Experiencing God Through Scripture*. Colorado Springs: NavPress, 1998.

Peterson, Eugene. *Eat This Book: A Conversation in the Art of Spiritual Reading*. Grand Rapids: Eerdmans, 2009.

Vest, Norvene. *Bible Reading for Spiritual Growth*. San Francisco: HarperSanFrancisco, 1993.

Chapter 6: Creation, Culture and Creativity

Detweiler, Craig. *Into the Dark: Seeing the Sacred in the Top Films of the 21st Century*. Grand Rapids: Baker Academic, 2008.

Detweiler, Craig, and Barry Taylor. *A Matrix of Meanings: Finding God in Pop Culture*. Grand Rapids: Baker, 2003.

Dyrness, William. *Poetic Theology: God and the Poetics of Everyday Life*. Grand Rapids: Eerdmans, 2011.

Johnston, Robert. *Reel Spirituality*. 2nd ed. Grand Rapids: Baker, 2006.

Wuthnow, Robert. *All in Sync: How Music and Art Are Revitalizing American Religion*. Berkeley: University of California Press, 2006.

———. *Creative Spirituality: The Way of the Artist*. Berkeley: University of California Press, 2001.

Chapter 7: Church

Bass, Dorothy C., ed. *Practicing Our Faith: A Way of Life for a Searching People*. San Francisco: Jossey-Bass, 1997.

Dawn, Marva J. *Reaching Out Without Dumbing Down: A Theology of Worship for the Turn-of-the-Century Culture*. Grand Rapids: Eerdmans, 1995.

Foster, Richard J. *Celebration of Discipline: The Path to Spiritual Growth*. San Francisco: Harper & Row, 1978.

Foster, Richard J., and Emilie Griffin. *Spiritual Classics: Selected Readings for Individuals and Groups on the Twelve Spiritual Disci-*

plines. San Francisco: HarperSanFrancisco, 2000.

Willard, Dallas. *The Spirit of the Disciplines: Understanding How God Changes Lives*. New York: Harper & Row, 1988.

Conclusion: How Do We Know It Is God?

Fryling, Alice. *Seeking God Together: An Introduction to Group Spiritual Direction*. Downers Grove, Ill.: InterVarsity Press, 2009.

Johnson, Ben Campbell. *Discerning God's Will*. Louisville: Westminster John Knox, 1990.

Morris, Danny E., and Charles M. Olsen. *Discerning God's Will Together: A Spiritual Practice for the Church*. Nashville: Upper Room Books, 1997.

Smith, Gordon. *Listening to God in Times of Choice: The Art of Discerning God's Will*. Downers Grove, Ill.: InterVarsity Press, 1997.

Notes

Epigraph

"The Merton Tapes," tape 8, side B, "Life & Solitude;" a talk given in 1965. The Thomas Merton Studies Center, Bellarmine College, Louisville, Ky., quoted in *Praying with Icons* by Jim Forest (Maryknoll, N.Y.: Orbis, 2008), pp. 51-52.

Introduction: How Do We Notice the Presence of God?

[1]See my book *Conversion in the New Testament: Paul and the Twelve* (Grand Rapids: Eerdmans, 1999) for my thinking on the subject.

[2]Diogenes Allen, *Spiritual Theology: The Theology of Yesterday for Spiritual Help Today* (Boston: Cowley Publications, 1997), pp. 2-3.

[3]Dallas Willard, *In Search of Guidance* (San Francisco: HarperSanFrancisco, 1993), p. 4.

[4]Gordon Mursell, ed., *The Story of Christian Spirituality: Two Thousand Years from East to West* (Minneapolis: Fortress, 2001), p. 9.

[5]I will be speaking a lot about God in this book. How to do so in the English language is a challenge. In English to speak about a person is to invoke gender. But God is neither male nor female. Mostly I will try not to use pronouns when referring to God, but it becomes quite tedious always trying to find a way around a pronoun. So, on occasion, I will refer to God as "he" or "him," just because that is the most common way of doing so.

[6]Ron Hansen, *Mariette in Ecstasy* (San Francisco: Harper Perennial, 1992), p. 174.

Chapter 1: Mystical Encounters

[1]Hugh T. Kerr and John Mulder, eds., *Famous Conversions* (Grand Rapids: Eerdmans, 1983), p. 37.

[2]William McCready, with Andrew Greeley, *The Ultimate Values of the American Population,* Sage Library of Social Research 23 (Beverly Hills, Calif.: Sage, 1976), p. 133.

[3]Andrew Greeley and William McCready, "Are We a Nation of Mystics?" *New York Times Magazine,* January 26, 1975, pp. 12-25.

[4]Tom W. Smith, "Spiritual and Religious Transformation in America: The National Spiritual Transformation Study," GSS Topical Report No. 37 (Chicago: NORC, 2005), p. 4. It needs to be noted that the 2005 study did not duplicate exactly the earlier study. No attempt was made to distinguish mystical experiences from other types of religious experience.

[5]Barbara Bradley Hagerty, *Fingerprints of God: The Search for the Science of Spirituality* (New York: Riverhead Books/Penguin, 2009), p. 150.

[6]Alister Hardy, *The Spiritual Nature of Man: A Study of Contemporary Religious Experience* (Oxford: Clarendon, 1979), p. 20.

[7]William James, *The Varieties of Religious Experience* (1902), Lectures 16 and 17.

[8]Tom Wright, *The Way of the Lord: Christian Pilgrimage Today* (Grand Rapids: Eerdmans, 1999), p. 5.

[9]C. S. Lewis, *The Weight of Glory and Other Addresses* (New York: Macmillan, 1949), chap. 2.

[10]C. S. Lewis, *Mere Christianity*, book 3, chap. 10.

[11]Hagerty, *Fingerprints of God*, p. 173.

[12]Ibid., p. 174.

[13]Ibid., p. 185.

[14]Ibid., p. 100.

[15]Ibid., pp. 77-78.

[16]Ibid. This is the theme of chapter 6.

[17]Ibid., pp. 276-77.

[18]Dr. Mario Beauregard of the University of Montreal Medical Center, cited in ibid., p. 241. See also Andrew Newberg and Mark Robert Waldman, *How God Changes Your Brain* (New York: Ballantine, 2010) for a very readable summary of their research related to neurological research and religious experience.

[19]Mother Teresa, *Come Be My Light: The Private Writings of the Saint of Calcutta*, edited and with commentary by Brian Kolodiejchuk, M.C. (New York: Doubleday, 2007), pp. 87-88.

Chapter 2: God in the Ordinary

[1]The Bible speaks of God as both "immanent" (present, accessible) and "transcendent" (hidden, totally beyond our reach, wholly Other). That both are true of God is part of the mystery of God.

[2]See Chris Lowney, *Heroic Leadership: Best Practices from a 450-Year-Old Company that Changed the World* (Chicago: Loyola Press, 2003), pp. 7-8, 57-59.

[3]Actually, Francis of Assisi was another unlikely spiritual pioneer. In his

youth, he too was a rich kid who was wild, irreligious, and preoccupied with the romance of knights and ladies.

[4]In 1978 Richard Foster published his seminal book *Celebration of Discipline* that served to alert many Protestants to the existence of this tradition.

[5]Eventually I wrote four small group guides (the Spiritual Formation Study Guides series) that sought to make available these practices to lay people: *Spiritual Journaling: Recording Your Journey Toward God* (1995); *Spiritual Autobiography: Discovering and Sharing Your Spiritual Story* (1998); *Contemplative Bible Reading: Experiencing God Through Scripture* (1996); and *Meditative Prayer: Entering God's Presence* (1998), all published by NavPress.

[6]This three-step version of the examen is described by George Aschenbrenner, S.J., "The Consciousness Examen," *Review for Religious* 31 (1972): 14-21.

[7]You can actually read the *Spiritual Exercises* on your own, and this does have some benefit. The translation that I found the most useful is *A Do-It-at-Home Retreat: The Spiritual Exercises of St. Ignatius of Loyola*, by André Ravier, S.J. (San Francisco: Ignatius Press, 1991). A newer and even more accessible version is Larry Warner, *Journey with Jesus: Discovering the Spiritual Exercises of Saint Ignatius* (Downers Grove, Ill.: InterVarsity Press, 2010).

[8]*The Jesuit Guide to (Almost) Everything: Spirituality for Real Life* (San Francisco: HarperOne, 2010), p. 1. This is the book to read if you want to know more about the Jesuits and Ignatian spirituality.

[9]Elizabeth Johnson, *Quest for the Living God: Mapping Frontiers in the Theology of God* (New York: Continuum, 2008), pp. 182-83; cf. Tertullian, *Against Praxeas*, 8.

Chapter 3: The Still Small Voice

[1]Dallas Willard, *In Search of Guidance: Developing a Conversational Relationship with God* (San Francisco: HarperSanFrancisco, 1993), p. 88. This book was later reissued as *Hearing God*.

[2]Ibid., p. 91.

[3]This is an experiment by Alain Aspect and colleagues described in Barbara Bradley Hagerty, *Fingerprints of God: The Search for the Science of Spirituality* (New York: Riverhead Books/Penguin, 2009), pp. 250-51.

[4]I asked David if he would write down this incident for me so I could share it with others since it was so striking. I am quoting here from that document.

[5]A rather famous book, *An Experiment in Time*, was published in 1927 by J. W. Dunne (republished in 1958 by Faber & Faber, in London) in which he describes a dream he had one night concerning the arrival in Sudan of an expedition of explorers who had trekked from South Africa. On the next day he discovered an article from the *Daily Telegraph* de-

scribing the very thing he dreamed. The book is a long reflection on the nature of pre-cognitive dreams. Nearer our own time, Kathryn Ann Lindskoog describes several striking pre-cognitive dreams she had in her book *The Gift of Dreams* (San Francisco: HarperCollins, 1979), pp. 111-16.

[6]See, for example, his statement in *Miracles* (chap. 5): "If we care to continue to make moral judgments (and whatever we say we shall in fact continue) then we must believe that the conscience of man is not a product of Nature. It can be valid only if it is an offshoot of some absolute moral wisdom, a moral wisdom, which exists absolutely 'on its own' and is not a product of non-moral, non-rational Nature" ([London: Fontana Books, 1964], p. 42). Lewis writes extensively about how the existence of convictions of right and wrong are evidence that God has implanted such a sense in our very core as humans made in God's image.

[7]"My Conversation with God," *Christianity Today,* March 2007, at www.christianitytoday.com/40658 (posted March 2, 2007).

[8]*Have Time and Be Free* (London: SPCK, 1965), pp. 29-32.

Chapter 4: The Power of Community

[1]Although this quotation is found in numerous places, as an online search will show, its origin is difficult to locate. Certainly Mother Teresa said this sort of thing on many occasions, though I am unable to find the place where she expressed it in this exact form. For examples of this idea, see *Mother Teresa: Essential Writings,* selected by Jean Maalouf (Maryknoll, N.Y.: Orbis, 2001), chap. 3.

[2]Esther de Waal, *Seeking God: The Way of St. Benedict* (Collegeville, Minn.: The Liturgical Press, 1984), pp. 19-20.

[3]Columba Stewart, O.S.B., *Prayer and Community: The Benedictine Tradition* (Maryknoll, N.Y.: Orbis, 1998), pp. 27-28.

[4]Ibid., p. 15.

[5]A wonderful resource for fixed-hour prayer, compiled by Phyllis Tickle, is titled *The Divine Hours* (New York: Doubleday, 2000; in various editions).

[6]Stewart, *Prayer and Community,* p. 32.

[7]*Rule of Benedict* 53.1. Interestingly, Benedict never uses the name Jesus. He always refers to Christ. "His Christology was 'high.' He speaks comfortably of Christ as God." Stewart, *Prayer and Community,* p. 28. In meeting Christ, we are meeting God.

[8]de Waal, *Seeking God,* p. 121.

[9]I am grateful to David Robinson for helping me grasp how Benedict understood the phrase "seeing Christ in others." The quotations and some of the ideas in this paragraph come from his email received on September 29, 2010.

See also the book by David Robinson, *Ancient Paths: Discover Christian Formation the Benedictine Way* (Brewster, Mass.: Paraclete Press, 2010).

[10]Stewart, *Prayer and Community,* p. 118.

[11]Mother Teresa, *Come Be My Light: The Private Writings of the Saint of Calcutta,* edited and with commentary by Brian Kolodiejchuk, M.C. (New York: Doubleday, 2007), p. 286.

[12]Andrew Greeley, *God in Popular Culture* (Chicago: Thomas More Press, 1988), p. 69.

[13]The way Gregory tells the story, the problem had to do with the unruly monks who refused to follow Benedict's more rigorous way of life. And indeed, when the plot was uncovered, Benedict did say, "God have mercy on you and forgive you," which is the response of a mature leader. Still, I wonder if the striking moderation of the *Rule* that he eventually wrote may be traced in part to his firsthand experience of the alienation that excessive strictness can bring?

[14]The translation by William Barclay of the phrase "works of the flesh," found in *The Letters to the Galatians and Ephesians* (Edinburgh: Saint Andrew Press, 1962), p. 50.

[15]Romans 12:6-8; 1 Corinthians 12:4-11, 27-31; Ephesians 4:11.

[16]David Robinson has written a most useful reflection on how to bring monastic principles into the life of a family: *The Busy Family's Guide to Spirituality: Practical Lessons for Modern Living from the Monastic Tradition* (New York: Crossroad, 2009).

[17]Romans 12 provides a wonderful description of the nature of Christian community.

Chapter 5: The Written Word

[1]Klaus Bockmuehl, *Listening to the God Who Speaks* (Colorado Springs: Helmers & Howard, 1990), p. 13.

[2]My doctoral work focused on discerning and describing the outline of Mark's Gospel. You can see what I came up with in part 2 of my book *Conversion in the New Testament: Paul and the Twelve* (Grand Rapids: Eerdmans, 1999).

[3]Barbara Bradley Hagerty, *Fingerprints of God: The Search for the Science of Spirituality* (New York: Riverhead Books/Penguin, 2009), pp. 71-72.

[4]Ibid., p. 72.

[5]Jennifer Howe Peace, from an unpublished reflection titled "Mapping God," 2011.

[6]This section is taken, in part, from Jeffrey Niehaus's *God at Sinai: Covenant & Theophany in the Bible and Ancient Near East* (Grand Rapids: Zondervan, 1995), which is a fascinating scholarly (but readable) discussion of God-appearances in the Bible.

[7]I am grateful to Elizabeth Johnson in her fine book *Quest for the Living God: Mapping Frontiers in the Theology of God* (New York: Continuum, 2008), p. 4, for drawing my attention to the phrase "God is a living God" in its biblical context.

[8]In fact, when I became a student at Fuller Theological Seminary I quickly got involved with a group of other students who had a vision for starting a new type of missionary organization in Africa (we called it African Enterprise). My wife and I worked with this group in Africa for eight years.

I do need to comment on the word *missionary,* which was common currency at that point in time. I am aware that it has come to have negative connotations related to a kind of cultural imperialism. And indeed during our years of work in Africa, a few of the missionaries were troubling (and troubled) individuals. On the other hand, some were among the finest people we knew, giving themselves tirelessly and selflessly to serve the needs of the poor and disadvantaged. Missionaries today are more comfortable thinking of themselves as "coworkers" with the church around the world.

[9]For more information about both group *lectio* and *lectio divina* in general, see my book *Contemplative Bible Reading* (Colorado Springs: NavPress, 1998).

Chapter 6: Creation, Culture and Creativity

[1]Susan Casey, *The Wave: In Pursuit of the Rogues, Freaks, and Giants of the Ocean* (New York: Doubleday, 2010), p. 184.

[2]Ibid., pp. 184-85.

[3]William Dyrness, *Poetic Theology: God and the Poetics of Everyday Life* (Grand Rapids: Eerdmans, 2011), p. 93.

[4]*Confessions* 7.7, cited in Elizabeth A. Johnson, *Quest for the Living God* (New York: Continuum, 2008), p. 198.

[5]Johnson, *Quest for the Living God,* p. 161; italics added.

[6]Gerard Manley Hopkins, "The Grandeur of God," in *Poems & Prose* (London: Penguin Classics, 1985).

[7]Dyrness, *Poetic Theology,* p. 23.

[8]Ibid., p. 92.

[9]Andrew M. Greeley, *God in Popular Culture* (Chicago: Thomas More Press, 1988), p. 9.

[10]Craig Detweiler and Barry Taylor, *A Matrix of Meanings: Finding God in Pop Culture* (Grand Rapids: Baker, 2003), p. 9.

[11]Ibid., pp. 16-17.

[12]Robert Johnston, *Reel Spirituality,* 2nd ed. (Grand Rapids: Baker, 2006), p. 13.

[13]Dyrness, *Poetic Theology,* p. 84, quoting Clive Marsh, "On Dealing with What Films Actually Do to People," in *Reframing Theology and Film: New*

Focus for an Emerging Discipline, ed. R. K. Johnston (Grand Rapids: Baker, 2007), pp. 147, 150.

[14]Greg Garrett, *The Gospel According to Hollywood* (Louisville: Westminster John Knox, 2007), p. xiii.

[15]Craig Detweiler, *Into the Dark: Seeing the Sacred in the Top Films of the 21st Century* (Grand Rapids: Baker Academic, 2008), p. 15.

[16]Ibid., p. 29.

[17]Music critic Jon Landau wrote in 1974: "I have seen rock and roll's future and its name is Bruce Springsteen." "The Harvard Square Theatre, Cambridge, Massachusetts, Presents Bruce Springsteen and the E Street Band, 9th May 1974," *The Real Paper,* May 22, 1974. Quoted in "Critic Declares Springsteen Future of Rock and Roll," on *Mass Moments* website, Massachusetts Foundation for the Humanities, ©2011, www.massmoments.org/moment.cfm?mid=138.

[18]Linda Randall, *Finding Grace in the Concert Hall: Community & Meaning Among Springsteen Fans* (Long Grove, Ill.: Waveland Press, 2011), p. 3.

[19]Ibid., p. 10.

[20]Ibid., p. 8.

[21]Jeremy Begbie argues that all three elements go into a sonic experience. It is not just musical sounds but musical practices (the interplay of sound and word) and musical settings (music making and music listening in a social and cultural setting) that form the power of music. "Music, Mystery and Sacrament," in *The Gestures of God,* ed. Geoffrey Rowell and Christine Hall (London: Continuum, 2004), pp. 173-91.

[22]Alexander McCall Smith, *The Charming Quirks of Others* (New York: Pantheon, 2010), p. 54.

[23]Ibid., pp. 59-60.

[24]John Updike, *Roger's Version* (New York: Fawcett Columbine, 1986), p. 14. A real life reflection on the evidence for God from a biological point of view is found in a book by Francis Collins, a pioneering medical geneticist who once headed the government Human Genome Project: *The Language of God: A Scientist Presents Evidence for Belief* (New York: Free Press, 2007).

[25]Updike, *Roger's Version,* p. 24.

[26]Billy Collins, "The Dead," in *Sailing Alone Around the Room* (New York: Random House, 2002), p. 33.

[27]Robert Wuthnow, *Creative Spirituality* (Berkeley: University of California Press, 2001), p. 262.

[28]Ibid.

[29]Ibid., p. 263.

[30]Dyrness, *Poetic Theology,* p. 19.

[31]Wuthnow, *Creative Spirituality,* p. 269.

[32]Ibid., p. 39.

[33]Johnson, *Quest for the Living God,* pp. 1, 8, 13-14.

[34]Meister Eckhart, "Apprehend God," in *Earth Prayers from Around the World,* ed. Elizabeth J. Roberts and Elias Amida (San Francisco: HarperSanFrancisco, 1991).

Chapter 7: Church

[1]Those born between 1984 and 2002.

[2]David Kinnaman and Gabe Lyons, *unChristian: What a New Generation Really Thinks About Christianity. . . . and Why It Matters* (Grand Rapids: Baker, 2007).

[3]Suffice it to say that as with any other institution, the church is indeed flawed since it is made up of flawed people living in a flawed world. This is no excuse for such inadequacies, but it does mean that the church must constantly be engaged in self-aware renewal, always striving to be what it is called to be.

[4]"Something perceptible by the senses which by Divine institution has the power both to signify and to effect sanctity and justice. . . . An outward sign of inward grace, a sacred and mysterious sign or ceremony, ordained by Christ, by which grace is conveyed to our souls." Daniel Kennedy, "Sacraments," *The Catholic Encyclopedia,* vol. 13 (New York: Robert Appleton Company, 1912), www.newadvent.org/cathen/13295a.htm.

[5]Here I am talking about adult baptism, of course. When parents bring infants for baptism, they stand in their stead as they bring their children to Jesus. Confirmation is the sacrament by which these children, when of age, accept the baptismal vows made on their behalf.

[6]The Book of Common Prayer (New York: Seabury Press, 1977), p. 423.

[7]Ibid., p. 499.

[8]Ibid., p. 491; quoting John 11:25-26 and Job 19:25-27.

[9]Ibid., p. 368.

[10]Matthew 26:26-29; Mark 14:22-24; Luke 22:14-20; 1 Corinthians 11:23-26.

[11]Lush Gjergji, *Mother Teresa: To Live, to Love, to Witness—Her Spiritual Way,* trans. Jordan Aumann, O.P. (Hyde Park, N.Y.: New City Press, 1995), p. 93.

[12]See my book that describes the process of writing and sharing a spiritual autobiography in a small group: *Spiritual Autobiography: Discovering and Sharing Your Spiritual Story* (Colorado Springs: NavPress, 1998).

[13]There is overlap between spiritual disciplines and spiritual practices, of course.

[14]See Dorothy Bass, ed., *Practicing Our Faith* (San Francisco: Jossey-Bass, 1997), pp. xi, 5.

[15]In chapter 4 I have discussed the way hospitality is expressed in monastic communities.

[16]From an email received December 21, 2010.

Conclusion: How Do We Know It Is God?

[1]Jon Krakauer, *Under the Banner of Heaven: A Story of Violent Faith* (New York: Doubleday, 2003), pp. 163-66.

[2]Ibid., p. 11.

[3]These three illustrations are taken from the thoughtful book by Ruth Tucker, *God Talk* (Downers Grove, Ill.: InterVarsity Press, 2005), chap. 1.

[4]Dallas Willard, *In Search of Guidance* (San Francisco: HarperSanFrancisco, 1993), p. 4.

[5]§175.

[6]A discussion of "consolation and desolation" is too complicated to include here. A wise spiritual director will offer us the guidance we need with this issue.

[7]André Ravier, S.J., *A Do-It-at-Home Retreat: The Spiritual Exercises of St. Ignatius of Loyola*, trans. Cornelius Michael Buckley, S.J. (San Francisco: Ignatius Press, 1991), p. 132.

[8]*The Book of Discipline of the United Methodist Church* (Nashville: Abingdon, 2004), p. 77.

[9]Barbara Bradley Hagerty, *Fingerprints of God: The Search for the Science of Spirituality* (New York: Riverhead Books/Penguin, 2009), pp. 63-64.

[10]Gerald May, *The Dark Night of the Soul: A Psychiatrist Explores the Connection Between Darkness and Spiritual Growth* (San Francisco: HarperSanFrancisco, 2004), pp. 64, 65.

[11]From an email received June 7, 2011, referring to C. S. Lewis's *The Great Divorce* where the narrator first arrives from hell/purgatory and discovers that heaven is so real that his feet are hurt by the grass because he is not yet sufficiently solid.

[12]Mother Teresa, *Come Be My Light: The Private Writings of the Saint of Calcutta*, edited and with commentary by Brian Kolodiejchuk, M.C. (New York: Doubleday, 2007), chaps. 8-11.

[13]Ibid., p. 185. Such a "dark night of the soul," according to St. John of the Cross, is the experience of many who walk in this way and is a sign of God's deep work within.